The Simple Man's
Burden

Observations
and Reflections
from Within
the Complex

The Simple Man's Burden

Observations
and Reflections
from Within
the Complex

Vergil Den

Aventine Press

Published by Aventine Press
750 State St. #319
San Diego CA, 92101
www.aventinepress.com

ISBN: 1-59330-700-4

www.vergilden.com

For my wife and family whom I love dearly.
Thank you for saving me and burning those damned suits.

TABLE OF CONTENTS

PROLOGUE

Back in high school, my religion teacher Mr. Carey had us read various works from Henry David Thoreau. Mr. Carey was much more of a philosopher than a religion teacher and, as one can imagine, quite the bane to the Christian Brothers that ran the preparatory school. Needless to say, Thoreau was not something you would typically read in religion class so you can appreciate the angst of the Brothers. But thank goodness Mr. Carey did not play by the rules.

Thoreau was introduced to me by a stroke of fate and his works remain with me today. "Walden" had the greatest impact, in particular the famous aphorism "The masses of men are living lives of quiet desperation." At sixteen, this vexed me and I found it hard to believe how any man would live his life in a way that would lead to desperation. My life was content and happy. I was physically fit and had a group of good friends. My days were filled with sport and leisure. I did more or less what I wanted to do (other than the chore of school).

So what did Thoreau mean by this? Not until my early thirties did I come to understand this – I came to realize it when I began to live it! Most people fall into a similar trap. We have tunnel vision when we define modern-day success – good paying job, higher education, nice car, big house, expensive dinners, and exotic vacations. By the time we realize where we are, it is too difficult to turn around – we are fat, immobile, aching, burdened by debt, and trapped in jobs we never wished to have.

The observations in this book are from a day in the life of a man who is living such a life and who has slowly recognized his grave situation over the years. His happenings have been collected from my years of experience in the business world. Obviously, all of these happenings did not occur in one day. In most cases, events that I write about are groupings of past events that together tell a meaningful story. Similarly, characters are not individuals per se, but generalizations and attributions across many individuals. Even the protagonist is a collection of many – e pluribus unum I suppose. As you will read, there are also numerous digressions and thought tangents as linear versus nonlinear is an underlying current in the book. This is manifested as the protagonist's stream of consciousness – with the occasional leap out of the head. I would like to think this book can be both fiction and nonfiction depending on your perspective. In the style of Diderot and his *Jacques the Fatalist & His Master* – is it satire, novella, conte? You may ask yourself the same questions after reading this book.

Regardless of the events and characters, it is ultimately the ideas put forth through them that are the most important. Given the protagonist's predicament, his reflections, not surprisingly, are dark and cynical. But he is heroic in his struggle to remain stoic (courageous, dignified, and wise) under the most absurd and frustrating modern-day circumstances – knowing that these circumstances are unlikely to change (and perhaps get worse). He is fatigued and has had little rest for his body, emotions, senses, and mind. This has placed an incredible burden on him. And it is this burden, the distance from his natural steady state, which he knows will only get greater given that there is little in modern life that can offset it. The only way to lift the burden is for him to make drastic changes in his life – to be in better accord with nature. He is aware of the Stoic Seneca, who went even a step further – which by no means do I recommend.

You may manage to pan some nuggets of wisdom, humor, and truth that marble through the text and across the chapters. They may offer a place for your mind to reflect on your journey to clarity and sanity. They have for me. This book, however, should not be considered a self-help book. I did not set out to provide answers to any of life's pressing questions. Nor did I set out to write a scientific study on humans and their behavior. What I aimed to do was to lay out some common absurdities that I have experienced or observed on topics such as business, fitness, food, and modern day-to-day living. I have to stress that actual observations and experience are the influencers of my thoughts and writing. I did not form some theory and set out to validate it. The birth of my daughter, high cholesterol, severe joint pain, limited mobility, the daily grind, death of family and friends, among other things, drove me to seek answers and to find evidence that acknowledged my sanity. What I found was enlightening in some cases and depressing in others. Fundamentally, I asked myself why I had not started this search earlier.

Mr. Carey and Thoreau were catalysts for me to begin my search. But a number of other thought leaders and pioneers in their field have guided me as I seek to reconcile my thoughts and experiences with the question, "Am I crazy?" Each influencer came as an "aha" moment in my life. A moment of clarity and recognition – a moment when I knew that what I was seeing or reading was true (or at least true to my common sense).

The Ultimate Fighter

In 1991, a young man named Royce Gracie appeared on the scene in a spectacle that was called the Ultimate Fighting Championship (UFC 1). It would include eight combatants from various martial arts concerns and pit them against one another to determine what art was in fact the most effective in combat. It was a no-holds-barred match-up in an eight-sided caged ring called the Octagon. A frail looking and unassuming young Brazilian named Royce would dominate the competition against men much larger and more menacing. Royce, the clear underdog, defeated three competitors without a punch thrown, in less than five minutes total. His system was known as Gracie Jiu-Jitsu or better known today as Brazilian Jiu-Jitsu (BJJ). In one event, Royce rendered a number of fighting arts, developed over hundreds of years, useless. I remember the feeling of seeing Royce and knowing instantly that BJJ was the best combat method for a small man to defeat a single larger opponent. It may perpetuate the ludic fallacy in some regard, but it is one of the very few martial arts that can be effectively applied to real-life situations.

Royce's skilled execution that night taught me two important life lessons. First, that there is hidden knowledge beyond what we can see and feel that fools our intuition and common sense. In this case, a large number of seemingly menacing men in battle with a frail (at least visually frail) teenager who just happened to be well versed in the most effective martial art of the day. The second life lesson is that effectiveness (or ineffectiveness) evolves over time. I am certain that the other martial arts were equally as effective as BJJ when they were first conceived (why else would they have been conceived?). Over time, however, they became obsolete for some reason – perhaps because the art evolved into sport, the type of opponent changed (effective only against a samurai with light armor), or other arts incorporated the most effective aspects of the art thus nullifying it. I am sure if BJJ does not innovate and adapt, it will become as ineffective as the obsolete arts it dominated during UFC 1. I hope it evolves.

The World's Fittest Man

We did not evolve to live in a world like we live in today. As adults (and more and more for children and adolescents) we live in a world that is foreign to every fiber in us that makes us human. Erwan Le Corre, a man whose ideas I discuss in this book, has coined this the Zoo Human condition. The quiet desperation we feel is the disconnect between our true nature and our modern condition. It is the distance between where we are and where we should be as humans. As we get farther and farther from our natural state, the more desperate we feel. Erwan took this idea and created a physical fitness movement based on human evolutionary principles to improve a person's health and well-being. It is called MovNat and the philosophy is built on three pillars: "Natural (like in any other animal, human biology is built upon natural laws that we cannot afford to overlook if we desire true and lasting health), Evolutionary (our bodies and minds are designed for the world of hundreds of thousands of years ago and both expect us to live like our ancestors), and Situational (the movements trained can always be linked to a practical application that justifies them)." [1] Erwan believes that movement is our evolutionary birthright. That movement is our nature; Nature is our movement. I believe it too.

The Notmilkman

My first daughter was born in January 2008. In the months leading up to her birth, I listened to discussions between friends and acquaintances about various parenting best practices such as the merits of breast-feeding over bottle-feeding. I never knew that this was even a question – why would anyone ever bottle-feed? It struck a chord with me because the answer seemed so obvious. How could what a scientist creates in a laboratory be better for an infant than what nature intended in a mother's breast milk? In my own independent research, I came across a gentleman named Robert Cohen, aka the Notmilkman.

He clearly puts the bottle-feeding fallacy to rest. But he continues on and challenges the common wisdom of drinking animal milk. In his book *Milk – The Deadly Poison*, his essays and research debunking, I came to rethink what I eat, what I do not eat, and the impact of modern food on the body and on society. I came to listen and trust the signals from my body. I also began my official journey into the thoughts and practices of skepticism. He regularly exposes the pseudoscience and deceptive marketing of the dairy industry. Robert is a tireless writer and shares a daily newsletter. I never fail to read one.

The Erudite

I typically can read through a good-sized book in a couple of hours. Most books are quick reads and one can pull out the salient points while speed reading. It is the rare book that requires one to stop, to savor, and to digest the nuggets of wisdom. Books like this often must be read three to four times to fully appreciate the wisdom. The last read is with great satisfaction, like when licking the plate from a wonderful meal and recognizing that you are satiated. This was the case when I read Nassim Taleb's *The Black Swan: The Impact of the Highly Improbable*. His theory on randomness and uncertainty helped organize my observations and experiences and formulate my thoughts around how humans behave in natural and unnatural settings. His ideas are humbling and have sparked in me a renewed joy in learning. I no longer read the newspaper and use the time to read books instead. I literally took Taleb's advice, "additional knowledge of the minutia of daily business can be useless, even actually toxic." I would recommend everyone at least try to stop listening to the news and reading the newspaper. Enjoy the peace and quiet.

I will end by noting that most of the topics addressed in this book use intuition and common sense as the primary means of support to either further the idea or to challenge conventional wisdom. Common sense (of the kind that is not warped) is a tool in the skeptic's tool belt and should be used to root out absurdities. I do not advocate using it in all cases, particularly when empirical support and scientific testing is required like in the case of quantum physics where common sense is dangerous and misleading. But common sense works well in matters of simple reason and logic – and in a book such as this.

I have also added some suggested reading and resources at the end of each chapter. It might appear that some sources contradict one another – sometimes they do. But a free thinker will consider everything and weigh the strengths and weaknesses accordingly. I have attempted to do this and I challenge you to do the same.

I hope that I have laid out some simple reasoning behind the absurdities that I have observed or experienced and perhaps that you, the reader, can relate to. At minimum, I hope this book acts as a catalyst to your own natural curiosity and desire for answers. Perhaps it even provides you a laugh or two. I immensely enjoyed writing this book. The work was much more satisfying than any work that I have ever done before. I hope you enjoy the fruits as much as I did the labor.

CHAPTER 1 - 6:17 AM – GROUND HOG DAY

"Give me control over a man's economic actions, and hence over his means of survival, and except for a few occasional heroes, I'll promise to deliver to you men who think and write and behave as I want them to." -- Benjamin A. Rogge

There is a certain tranquil stillness in the early morning hours – almost as if you are the only person in existence. Not like at night where there remains a gentle humming – a remnant of the day's happenings still lingering in the air. At dawn, the day is fresh. The only sounds are yours. Yet it is during these moments when we realize that every day is not a clean slate. We are tethered to the past and all its noise. Soon others will come along and further taint the day with their chatter. The day is to be shared with everyone and everything without compromise – the good and the bad. And so every day begins like the last.

I just could not motivate myself to work out this morning. Not even some light stretching. When the days get shorter and grayer, I find it difficult to motivate myself to do anything. This could be a byproduct of years of evolution. Melancholy (or depression at its worst) would have helped my ancestors stay inside their caves or primitive dwellings during harsh winters – or so I like to believe. Or maybe my lack of motivation is a byproduct of this path that I chose and knowing of the long road that lies ahead – a kind of numbing as a survival technique against modern realities. Perhaps this numbing has numbed more than I wanted, impacting the things I enjoy – like exercising.

I will have to find some workaround because I need the numbing. I know intuitively that this daily ritual is not what I am designed to do and numbing seems to help. I used to be energized, invigorated by the uncertainty that lay ahead. What does not kill you makes you stronger, I used to think. This may be true of an athlete training for an event. But it is not true of poison, disease, or just falling off a cliff, breaking your neck, and surviving. It is an adage of the wishful thinker or of the inexperienced one who wants to convince himself to take a risk. Most people end up at least a bit weaker – both physically and mentally – from those things that do not kill them. I suppose I am a pessimist. I should probably project a more positive attitude – Tony Robbins style. Perhaps some upbeat thoughts will make it easier. But I know that is not true – it was optimism that got me here in the first place. I will just do it like I have always done. I do it without complaint – without emotion. I will be patient and disciplined. Just another day to get through.

I take a deep breath – breathing in through my nose by expanding my stomach, breathing out through my mouth by contracting my stomach. The air is cool and heavy – wet almost – and there is a hint of an active fireplace in the air. The smell of wood burning is a comforting smell. It is a smell of childhood campfires. Even when the smoke would waft in my direction, I would sit and embrace it – knowing the smell would be embedded in the fibers of my plaid jacket and corduroy pants. I could take the essence with me and enjoy it for later. I wonder if the smell of wood burning is seared into our genes as a primal reminder of our life when we were just a whisker away from the chimp. The smell just feels so right.

I can hear the distant rumbling of the bus in the east. I turn to see and I am instantly blinded by the rising sun. As the bus nears, it blocks the sun like the moon does during a solar eclipse. I never rode the bus before commuting to the city. I had this middlebrow aversion to it. The subway has a certain danger that is appealing. But the bus – it is just so Ralph Kramden. I got over it when I realized I had no other choice. I had to commute this way. Actually, the bus is just one component of my commute. I am living in the movie *Planes, Trains and Automobiles*. How did it ever come to be that I would suffer a two-hour commute? Car to bus – bus to train – train to city – walk to office. How did I get here?

The bus pulls up a few feet in front of where I stand. I climb the stairs and insert my metro card into the card reader. After a few attempts, and a couple of rearrangements of how I insert the card, the machine accepts me and beeps with success. But all I hear is the buzz of failure. Like that awful buzz from the game of Operation - when the tweezers touch the metal attempting to remove the breadbasket.

The bus is standing room only. There is a collection of men and women of all shapes, sizes, races, and ethnicities. The common factor is profession. I suspect everyone works for a bank and is a compliance officer, journeyman attorney, accountant, or back-office operations manager. You can tell a person's professional level by his garb – particularly the shoes. This group wears the unpolished sneaker type that is good for walking but not for first impressions.

Among these frumps is the outlier – in this case, the well dressed old man in the back of the bus. He is in his late seventies at least. You can faintly tell that he was handsome in his younger days but time, among other things, has relegated his good looks to a place for dusty photos. He is impeccably dressed but his suit is ill fitting – so big that it appears almost to consume him. It is curious that most old people appear to shrink over time, perhaps a natural symptom from years of gravity or an unnatural symptom from years of jobs. Work is good – a job is not. I hope the old man really needs the money for no other reason than to save him from disgrace. There is nothing more pitiful than a wealthy old man who has only his job to love.

A general quiet hovers amongst the thirty odd people. Everyone is in a daze as if no one has either fully woken up or fully resigned to the fact that this day is like the previous and the next – like Bill Murray in *Groundhog Day*. We rumble along, stopping periodically to scoop up the wayward commuter. The bus pulls up at the last stop and drops us off at the train station. The station itself is set high above the tracks and the platform. A number of us sprint to the Starbucks. It sits where there was once a small newspaper and coffee stand.

There is a long line. Starbucks is particularly frustrating to someone who simply wants a cup of black coffee. It used to be that is all anyone ever wanted. The cappuccino, latte, and their variations were the domain of small Italian or French cafes. Americans just liked either plain old black coffee or light and sweet. Now the options are limitless – there must be thousands of different combinations. I am not sure if the lines are longer because of all the choices and the time needed to render each option, or if more people are drinking coffee and they happen to have chosen my Starbucks to order their brew.

I like my coffee. It is one of the few vices I have yet to kick. It is something I look forward to in the morning. It is a treat for me, a way to satisfy the need for caffeine. The caffeine that gives me a pop. The pop I need because of the numbness – to help compensate for the poor sleep – the fatigue. A crutch, I suppose, and one of the few vices I have left to kick.

I know coffee is not the best thing for me. Yet I continue to drink it. It is curious how we can know so many things with the utmost certainty and yet act against them. This contradiction is everywhere. We have been given the facts about smoking, yet continue to smoke. We have seen *Fast Food Nation*, yet continue to eat fast food. This afflicts even the most educated, the most esteemed. Sure, some of this can be attributed to physical addiction or cultural norms. I suspect some choose to ignore the facts. Most, however, choose to act against their reason. It is a self-destructive counterbalance to our reason that put us here in the first place when we reasoned with ourselves and accepted this world. A world that we designed but one that we were not designed for.

Suggested Reading/Resources

The Wisdom of Insecurity: A Message for an Age of Anxiety

BY ALAN W. WATTS

Good central concept of reverse effort. Alan argues that in order to be more secure, one needs to recognize and accept that insecurity is inseparable from life. The less you fight it, the happier you will be.

CHAPTER 2 - 6:42 AM – SCIENCE AS FICTION

"...man will occasionally stumble over the truth, but usually manages to pick himself up, walk over or around it, and carry on."
-- Winston S. Churchill

The train arrives at the station. As it pulls up, the crowd slowly shifts, anticipating where exactly a door for one of the train cars will stop and open. There does not seem to be any logic to the train operator's actions. On some days, he pulls up in exactly the same spot as the day before. On other days, it is a few feet forward from the previous day. And still on other days, it is a few feet back from the previous day. I notice that most commuters seem to think there is some pattern to it. I suspect some use a marker of sorts. I have observed a number of commuters try to line themselves up with a marker hoping in anticipation that they have solved the equation. It rarely works. When the train door stops in a different location, they chalk this up to an anomaly. They continue to resume the behavior the next day. I even found myself falling into this trap of thinking. At best, it helps to pass the time.

The train stops. As the doors open, we slowly corral ourselves onto the train, all hoping to get a seat. We pay too much in monthly fees to have to stand for over an hour. A slight drizzle begins to fall from the sky. This creates a bit of frenzy and people begin a stampede. Fortunately, there are enough seats and the crush slowly dissipates. I am one of the last to board.

I scan the car for an open seat. I see rows and rows of depressed commuters. Some have their eyes closed. Most are reading either the *Times* or *Journal.* The remaining few are locked in with the thousand-mile stare – shell-shocked for sure.

I find a seat in the rear train car. I sit and place my coffee on the floor next to me. I hope no one kicks it over. Every morning there is at least one cup of coffee that is spilled inadvertently on the train. The ooze slowly makes it way from one end of the car to the other – like a toxic spill. It divagates under seats, straight down the aisle, sometimes breaking left or right seemingly for no apparent reason. Bags on the floor from unsuspecting commuters are the victims – no less an unpleasant surprise when we reach Grand Central Station. Black coffee is forgivable. It is really just colored water. A cappuccino or another milk laden drink is not. Shortly after the spill, the milk festers, gets sour, grows mold, and reeks of foulness.

There are the typical advertisements on the billboards situated in the clear panels that separate the front and rear of the train car from the middle of the car. I notice one peculiar advertisement. It reads, "Walk for a cure" (presumably breast cancer because of the pink lettering). This is very puzzling indeed. Why do they walk to find a cure instead of walking to find prevention? Everyone gets "gung-ho" for these walks. Participants form teams and wear T-shirts, bandanas, and all kinds of flair. There is so much energy one might mistake it for homecoming or a tailgate but without all the booze. I usually get four or five emails from friends requesting a small donation, friends who have lost a family member to cancer.

I am empathetic to their cause given my mother died from breast cancer. I usually donate something but I never feel good about it. I find it hard to believe that there is a silver bullet to the cancer problem. The human is not a machine – we are complex. If all of that research money (both philanthropic and for-profit) was shifted to prevention, I am sure cases of cancer would become statistically immaterial. But alas, all those scientists, bureaucrats, and executives would be jobless. There is a very profitable market for these "cures" which is a good incentive to keep people sick. And keep people sick they do – at least until they eventually succumb. The testimonials of those that have been cured by one of these cancer drugs or treatments would lead you to believe that most remiss. Where is the "Tell-Tale Heart" that speaks for the silent – for the victims – those that the drug did nothing for except raise hope and prolong suffering. They have no testament.

To be fair, there have been some preventative areas that have recently gained press. There is now testing among women for the BRCA gene. BRCA is the gene that supposedly predisposes women to breast cancer. After testing positive for this gene, many women out of fear have, with the consent and counsel of their physicians, decided to self-mutilate – to have their breasts removed.

This goes beyond just breast cancer preventative care. I recently met with my doctor for my annual physical, and she saw in my family health history a report that my mother had breast cancer. She strongly recommended that I see a doctor who specializes in cancer genetics to see if I had a genetic predisposition to prostate cancer. She said, at minimum, it would help me to be informed. I wonder what she meant by informed. What do you do with this information? Perhaps if they find this gene marker, my prostate should be removed – perhaps the lower half of my body? Is this where science has gone – to remove offending appendages when there is no clear evidence of cause and effect – not even a strong correlation? Is this the evolution of the enlightenment? If so, give me prayer and fasting instead. The logic and science of medicine is so unsound.

A middle-aged woman sits next to me on the train. I always take an aisle seat, as it affords a quicker exit. Between our seats spans the unpopular middle seat that plagues all passenger vehicles – the seat of last avoidance if you will. On planes you have no choice if assigned a middle seat and in taxis or cars, only the lowest of individuals sit there. On trains most commuters would prefer to stand than to sit in the middle seat – only the arrogant, handicapped, or first-ride amateurs ever sit there. So even though the train is racing toward Grand Central during this morning's rush, only our bags occupy this seat (much better than on the floor). The woman is munching on some yogurt granola concoction, no doubt believing she is eating something that is healthy. And why not? Recent reported studies suggest dairy consumption will cure all ailments. I am sure she has not read the studies, of course; who reads those things? Most read only the vignette in some health magazine highlighting the calcium benefits of dairy or some other rubbish..

There are numerous unreported studies that are not in the magazines that tell a different story. The story is that there is a strong correlation between dairy consumption and a number of diseases. In the case of milk and cancer, the logic is simple. Mother's milk of all different mammals contains similar growth hormones. In humans and in cows, these hormones are identical. Both contain seventy amino acids in the identical sequence. This is the only known example in nature in which one identical hormone is shared by two species. In humans, this hormone is called insulin-like growth factor one (IGF-1). These growth hormones enhance growth and development. This is important for infants for obvious reasons. Adults consuming milk and other dairy products also absorb these growth hormones (IGF-1 survives stomach acidity in both babies and adults because it is buffered with casein and fat molecules). These growth hormones encourage normal cell growth in both infants and adults. Besides stimulating growth of normal cells, they also stimulate growth of cells that have been damaged or mutated. Over time, the number of damaged or mutated cells increases. Therefore, the more milk and dairy one consumes, the more mutated and damaged cells are available to catalyze and grow.

Non-milk dairy products concentrate the load of growth hormones. It takes twelve pounds of milk to make one pound of ice cream and ten pounds of milk to produce one pound of hard cheese. Eating these foods only increases the delivery of growth hormones. By consuming dairy one's body will grow – both the good (muscles) and the bad (cancerous cells).[2]

Although the logic and supporting science are clear, I think they have been ignored because it would be too inconvenient for individuals to change their behavior. Think about all the pizzas you would need to stop eating. No more cookies and milk. No more buttered toast. No more macaroni and cheese. No more ice cream on a hot summer's day. Dairy treats have been seared into our culture – our history – our memory pathways. Even my two-year-old is conditioned to salivate upon hearing the jingle from the Mr. Softee ice cream truck.

We as human have the reason to break these conditions but we continue to delude ourselves with weak excuses. Take for example the smoker. A person smokes for a number of reasons against all logic and reason. Aside from those that are physically dependent, why do people continue to smoke? As a former smoker, I remember deluding myself and others deluding themselves in a number of ways.

1. I am going to die anyway – so who cares.

2. I will stop soon (or I am young so I have time), so no worries.

3. My grandmother (or some other close and deceased relative) smoked and lived to 100 (or some freakish old age) and so will I.

4. It helps me think better (or relax) and so my success or happiness depends on it.

5. I smoke only in social situations like when drinking at the bar, so it doesn't impact me given the limited number of times I smoke.

6. I will do whatever I want to do (or I think the science is wrong).

I suspect, given the smoking analogy, that the "Got Milk" denial is a combination of both delusion on the part of the individual and something more sinister; perhaps people are just ignorant of the facts and have not had an opportunity to choose. Perhaps the question should not be why has it been ignored but rather, why has it not been more publicized? Why is there pseudoscience supporting the increased consumption of dairy? You will be able to find research supporting the increased consumption of dairy just as you could have found forty years ago why smoking causes no harm. You must use your own bullshit detection toolkit to find the answer. But like every popular myth or common knowledge debunked, people first laugh, then they get angry (very angry), and then they accept. I suspect in the case of dairy, we are entering the angry phase.

I want to calmly speak to this woman and warn her of the dangers. My sense tells me otherwise. She may get defensive, and I do not like to argue as it takes an enormous amount of effort, and in most cases, offers little reward. I prefer to simply ask provocative questions and hope that the responses I receive, regardless of quality, add to my collective knowledge. I am an introvert and perhaps it is my predisposition to avoid conflict, so I keep my mouth shut, particularly when it comes to a sensitive subject like dairy. People have a violent tendency to defend it, using the most illogical rants, reacting like I have insulted their mother. Dairy holds a special place that is near and dear to many people. I suppose it is because the dairy marketers have ingrained in us that, along with our right to free speech, every American has a right to a glass of milk. I think I may have even read this claim in one of those ubiquitous "Got Milk" mustaches ads.

Needless to say, the more she munches, the more frustrated I get and the more I focus on the munching. It is very irritating and difficult to ignore. I need to shift my attention. I wish people would just eat their food in their homes or some food establishment. There are always a few individuals who insist on eating on the train and violating their neighbor's sensibilities. The train ride home is particularly offensive. It never fails that some Empty Suit is drinking a beer and munching on a hot dog – a snack before dinner perhaps – munch – silence – burrrppppp– munch – silence – burrrpppp.

It has been fifteen years that I have been working in the city. I had promised myself when I entered the workforce that I would not work in the city. It drove my father mad. I would have preferred to work in an executive park with the sprawling parking lots, horizon-friendly buildings, and well landscaped grounds. I reaffirmed this after 9/11, but ten years later, nothing has changed.

It is funny about all those promises we made to ourselves after 9/11. You know the ones how family would come first, how we would work to live rather than live to work. But 9/11 was just like a bad cold for most bystanders – a momentary lapse of health and all that comes with it – the frantic prayers, promises of change, slow recovery, recognition of relief, and business as usual. You would think these moments would be seared into our psyche and change our behavior. But they do not. Think about the cancer survivor who continues to smoke or the diabetic who continues to drink. It defies all reason – how soon we forget and how great our ability to delude ourselves. In life, we continue to push ourselves to acquire more, whether it is the currency of money, recognition, respect, or hope. But in the process, we also fail to calculate (or to properly calculate) the tradeoff. I cannot help but feel that I am stuck on a treadmill and cannot get off.

The woman next to me finally finishes her yogurt parfait concoction. She is struggling with what to do with the remains of her meal. She stuffs her napkin in the plastic cup with the spoon and wedges it between herself and the train wall. Out of sight, out of mind.

The train is passing 125th Street and already the Empty Suits are getting up from their seats and positioning themselves as first to exit the train. I am convinced these people need their fix – they go to work to medicate them-selves knowing that they have sacrificed so much for a big paycheck. A vicious circle. As we whisk through uptown New York, I remember when gutted buildings used to permeate the landscape. Many of these have been renovated or are in the process of being renovated (most are stalled renovations given that money has dried up since the great recession). I also imagine all the bank branches and the dollar stores on street level and their clueless customers.

I see in the distance my doctor's buildings. The Upper Eastside is a kind of Silicon/Hodgkin Alley. If you have an affliction, they have a doctor. I have become very wary of doctors over the years. They are my fallen heroes. Medicine is great but individual doctors are dangerous. Perhaps it is the cost and debt from years of school and training that has jaded them. Whatever the reason, they seem to be just as delusional as the next guy. Let me share the following experience (it is just one of many absurdities that I have experienced with doctors). A few years ago, I suffered a shoulder injury in my judo class. I was not sure if my shoulder was separated or if I had a broken collar bone. I just knew that my shoulder had significantly less mobility than it did before the fall and it really hurt. Prudently, I went to an orthopedic surgeon. He was significantly overweight which concerned me. Was he not aware of all of the research on obesity? Surely as a doctor he was informed. As I found out, he was informed, but of the misinformed kind.

He offered me two superbly stupid recommendations. Firstly, it was deter-mined from the x-ray that I had only a slight clavicle separation. Yet he told me that, to prevent this type of injury in the future, I needed to drink more milk to strengthen my bones.

The science is out there that shows that milk has no positive effect on bone health. Quite the opposite. Moreover, my bone was not even injured. Yet he offered this ridiculous recommendation. My guess is that he was clearly deluded by the slogan "Milk – It does a body good" and all of its supporting science – the same science that finds a correlation between reduction in breast cancer rate and increased smoking. He then went on to tell me that as an adult I should not be doing this kind of exercise – the kind of exercises that children do. He recommended spinning (also known as exercising on a stationary bike) as an alternative. As someone who sits all day long, I do not look forward to another second in my day that requires sitting. I also do not wish to waste my energy pedaling on a bicycle that does not move.

It was the "children" comment that really struck me as odd. When children exercise, they play. When they play, they are exercising. They are not decoupled activities – they are one and the same. Somewhere along the line, someone (probably some Empty Suit doctor or scientist) determined that adult exercise should not be playful – or fun for that matter – and separated play from exercise. I suspect it was the same person who invented the stationary bike. Needless to say, neither did I take the doctor's recommendations nor did I visit him again.

The train finally arrives at Grand Central Station. The platform is a chaotic mess of people hurriedly trying to get to work faster than their neighbor – some heading to the main concourse, others in the opposite direction to the 47th Street Cross Passage. The air is musty with the smell of heavy diesel fuel and there is a deafening sound emanating from a lead locomotive on the adjacent track. Water is dripping from high above from leaks in the ceiling concrete. A few individuals remain on the train. I hope they wake up or they may find themselves on an express train back North.

I lug my work bag as if it were an albatross but around my shoulder rather than my neck. The bag contains my computer, power cord, a bunch of steno pads, and miscellaneous technology knickknacks. The days of the briefcase have been over for some time and perhaps even the computer bag is on that route. We are burdened with work now more than ever and many treat it like a prized possession. So I suppose it is only natural that the trend is shifting to roll one's work bag as if it were luggage. But do not be fooled. Although the bag is easier to transport, rolling does not lessen the hazard of the contents to the owner's health. And it can be equally hazardous to the unsuspecting pedestrian – not so much the contents but the bag itself. It never fails that at least one person trips over these things. They may be common at airports but are not yet ubiquitous in Grand Central Station for people to unconsciously avoid.

After some time of this human herding, I reach the main concourse. Every day, the first thought that crosses my mind is why the terrorists have not attacked Grand Central. Grand Central seems like such low hanging fruit. I imagine that there are snipers perched in hidden causeways or that MTA ticket agents are in fact U.S. Special Operations commandos ready to take action. Maybe the terrorists know this and therefore will not attack. Maybe the terrorists did try to attack, and the attack was thwarted. I suppose we will never know.

Suggested Reading/Resources

Milk - The Deadly Poison

BY ROBERT COHEN

www.notmilk.com

Exposes false claims and science supported by the dairy industry and offers insights into the influence the dairy industry has within government. Robert offers a free daily informative newsletter on the negative health implications of dairy that can be found at http://health.groups.yahoo.com/group/notmilk

Wrong: Why Experts Keep Failing Us—And How to Know When Not to Trust Them

BY DAVID H. FREEDMAN

Exposes false claims made by experts, from respected economists to scientists, and the magnitude of the problem. Along with this book, I recommend reading his article in the November 2010 issue of *The Atlantic* called "Lies, Damned Lies, and Medical Science." "Much of what medical researchers conclude in their studies is misleading, exaggerated, or flat-out wrong. So why are doctors—to a striking extent—still drawing upon misinformation in their everyday practice? Dr. John Ioannidis has spent his career challenging his peers by exposing their bad science." www.theatlantic.com/magazine/archive/2010/11/lies-damned-lies-and-medical-science/8269/

Chapter 3 - 8:09 AM – Of Atrophy and Hypertrophy

"Men have become tools of their tools." -- Henry David Thoreau

I exit Grand Central Station and make my way over to the office. The buildings are imposing and suffocating. Even after years of working in the city, I cannot get past the fear that something will fall from the sky – perhaps shards of glass. I am somewhat validated in my fear given that this has happened before but the odds of it occurring are remote. More unlikely, but even more frightening, is getting hit by a falling penny. The urban legend of someone dropping a penny off of the Empire State building has never left me. I cannot get over it regardless of how much I reason with myself. Would it just go right through me?

There is a light rain – so light that the umbrella vendors have not yet popped up their transient carts with price gouging shoddy umbrellas. But undoubtedly hard enough that the collective stupidity of New York will increase and everything from subways to sandwich shops will be running slower. This is what I call the unpleasant weather condition effect. It could be caused by the many pedestrians who lack any self-awareness and choose to use golf umbrellas when walking on the sidewalk.

I think this effect is similar in most cities given that people in the big cities have lost their common sense. Rain is something to be feared and avoided – it ruins the best suits and dresses. We have been so conditioned to see the unnatural that we lack appreciation and awareness of the natural. I suspect the nearest thing to nature most city kids get to experience is a city park. That is if they can escape the comfort of their couches and cookies. It has gotten so absurd that money is spent on scientific studies to demonstrate the benefits of seemingly obvious things such as exercising outdoors.

One study found that natural environments can help you feel healthier. [3] One would think that this is common sense. But our common sense has become so skewed that perhaps these studies are helpful. Heaven forbid the shirtless man who runs on the grass, jumps off rocks and climbs trees – he is liable to be shot. A morbidly obese man in an athletic suit running on a treadmill watching television does not even turn one head.

The rain begins to change from a drizzle to a downpour. I choose to open my Unbreakable Umbrella. It is not a golf umbrella – no, it serves a higher purpose. It really can split a melon – much more useful and much less ubiquitous. Needless to say, I too have been conditioned to dislike the rain. I am just better outfitted.

I enter my office building and the usual security guard is acting as the sentinel. The guard just waves me through with a smile as I wave at him some random badge I found in my work bag. I have found you are better screened at your local Costco or Sam's Club than in most office buildings. It is interesting that, since 9/11, all the buildings and public spaces in New York City have erected these facades of increased security. But frankly, they are nothing but a nuisance and a time waster to ordinary working New Yorkers. They can be penetrated by the most elementary of techniques and are effective only at scaring little children. If they will not do it right then they should not do it at all. This false sense of security is only fooling the fools.

I head up to my office via the elevator. I have this sense of dread that I cannot shake. It could be mistaken for the Monday morning blues or for fear of elevators but I think it is my sense warning me of the perils in the office. It is dangerous sitting all day in a sterile environment – or perhaps not so sterile, as the air is toxic from anything ranging from toner dust to eletrosmog. My keyboard for sure is more hazardous to my health then a Bryant Park toilet. But it is the sitting that I dread. One should not be in a seat all day. Sitting is such an awkward and unnatural position.

Death by white collar can come in many forms but perhaps the worst is the rigid death – where one's joints become stiff and muscles atrophied from sitting. It is ironic that there once was a time when being white collar was something to be envied. It was the blue collar jobs that were less appealing. The reverse holds true today in a sense. Many at least get to move. For the blue collar workers that also happen to be unionized (particularly the civil servants), they hold the keys to the middle class. Guaranteed employment with a pension is the Holy Grail in today's economy.

The elevator arrives at my floor. I make my way to my office but take a detour to get a cup of Keurig coffee. My calendar today is relatively open except for a client meeting in the afternoon. I walk to my office and I pass the rows of empty cubicles peppered with the occasional associate. Almost like a call center, I suppose, but with more educated staff. Most days are like this – some days you may see no one except the occasional executive assistant. The mood is the typical gray. I miss the days of the dotcom bubble when there was excitement in the air and the air of creativity – the few days when technologists ruled the world. Even a poorly designed web page (the kind with the marbled background) would elicit the most envious "oohs" and "ahhs." Two burst bubbles later, and now the riskoligists and compliancists run the world, or at least that is what Empty Suits want us to believe.

I reach my desk. I sit in a small office with no windows. The office placard has been replaced with an index card with my name – someone removed it some time ago and it has yet to be substituted with anything official. It makes me feel like Milton from *Office Space*. Perhaps I was fired and was never informed.

I think squatting in my office is worse than if I were in a cubicle. In a cubicle, one is at least grazing with the other beasts. One can communicate with a simple grunt. I, on the other hand, am in a prison cell – surrounded by only white walls and faux light – light so white you can almost see the flicker from the florescent bulbs. If you consciously focus on the flicker too long you are bound to have an epileptic seizure. How great is our unconscious mind, to filter out such annoyances and distractions as little flickers. But at what cost – this small effort overtime must have an exponentially great toll.

I boot up my laptop. It takes a while to start up and I just sit and wait. One would think that with every advancement in processing power and computing speed, the time it takes to boot a computer would improve. But that is not the case. It seems that there is a linear relationship between these advancements in technology and total time wasted – a steady state of sorts. It does not improve or degrade. It fails to move – probably the result of a net effect between technology improvement and bloat.

On my desk is a stack of my accomplishments. It contains reports that I have drafted over the years and technical essays that I have written (horribly edited of course by copy editors and risk managers). God forbid we write something thought provoking. A torn and fading cartoon of *Bloom County* is pinned to the backboard – an older one when Opus and Bill the Cat actually shared the spotlight with Oliver, Steve, Binkley, and Milo. It illustrates Opus trying to pick up a barbell. He loses balance and control, then bounces down the stairs into the prairie toward Milo and Binkley. The last caption reads: "This unfortunate affair was to end suddenly down in Miller's Mud Flats with some injury. And while events were marked with general chaos, it was, nevertheless, apparent to all that the 'Schwartzeneggerization' of Opus was simply not to be." Above me on my shelf are awards from various projects where my team has been recognized by a client for our performance. Little trophies to this life I suppose but little more than chotchkies.

A picture of my wife and children on the beach is the only sign of life in the office, a static reminder of where I should be. I stare and wish to be in the picture. Ah yes, the beach with my family. I can almost hear the laughter, the crash of the waves, and white noise from sea foam – the smell of the sea brine – the sun's cleansing heat on my skin penetrating deep into my blood. I quickly pull myself back to the now. It can be dangerous to dream at work. Only in B horror films can one transcend into pictures. At work, one can only regret. I feel a certain sadness that I cannot quite pinpoint and is difficult to articulate. I shake it off.

Once my computer boots up, I'm all set to go. I open up to my email. My inbox is littered with all kinds of mail. Some work-related but most not. Of interest is the peppering of LinkedIn invitations. The ones from colleagues are hints into the sender's future plans with the firm. If you set a thirty-day clock, at thirty-one days most will have moved on to greener pastures. There is also a message from our CEO. I wonder what it could be. Perhaps a reorganization or a rebranding. The subject line reads "Office of the Chief Executive: A Message from Bradley McRandlesmith."

> "I wanted to extend a sincere thank you to all of our staff and managers for the great effort you put forth everyday in delivering value to our customers. You have a commitment to excellence, and you demonstrate it by living our firm's high performance culture. As a firm, we will continue to focus our efforts on executing our strategic priorities and our team will be well-positioned to fully achieve our vision. We must be willing to push ourselves beyond our comfort zones, take calculated risks and support one another. You know your career needs and aspirations best. We encourage you to take ownership for what you want to accomplish personally and professionally, and help drive us all toward our strategic goals."

This is very interesting email indeed. Not the content per se – this is just typical leadership jargon that upon further dissection literally means absolutely nothing. But figuratively, this email is of great consequence. I suspect layoffs in the near future. These messages always precede a negative event. I find them particularly cruel given all the unsuspecting fools who read this and believe it is in fact sincere. They will be the turkeys. The ones who have been fed stellar performance reviews and whose egos have been plumped up by praise and undeserved credit. The butcher is sharpening his cleaver and he will roast the fattened. One must learn to read between the lines in business.

I am interrupted by a colleague of mine, Paul Masterson, who casually wanders into my office. Paul is most recognizable by his full head of hair (not a gray or bald spot to be found) and his muscular physique (he can be considered what they call in the New Jersey vernacular a "musclehead"). He is well schooled (Harvard MBA) but lacks the sophistication one would think is inherent in a graduate of such a school. I suspect his father may have pulled a few strings. It is not uncommon at these elite colleges – particularly when one has deep pockets and a highbrow family lineage. Paul, for all of his background, is just a simple man. If I met him on the street, I would have guessed that he was a high-school baseball coach.

Paul is clearly concerned as he must have concluded the same as I from McRandlesmith's email. His concern quickly morphs into curiosity of the gossip kind – what will be the criteria for the reduction in workforce (business jargon for layoffs), who will be the first to go, when will this happen, what will be the severance. I offer him little satisfaction because I just do not know. I know the event will probably happen but the details are beyond my range of knowledge. It could be me for all I know.

This is something I had often thought of and have prepared for. Anyone in business should be prepared for such an event – resume primed, network connected, and most importantly, a stuffed cash pillow or two. It is curious how layoffs are so common in business (we are employed at will and can be sacked at a moment's notice) yet so many people are unprepared when it happens. They think, "It happens but it won't happen to me." These are the same people who have homeowner's insurance – with an umbrella policy no less. Next thing you know, they are out of a job and immediately operating on a line of credit. Why they are prepared for some unexpected events and not others escapes me. Losing one's job can happen to anyone at any moment and for no good reason. Alas, even the Empty Suits are not immune!

This, along with some of physical ailments, seems to be stressing on Paul. His ailments are not a condition of his genetics, poor diet, or his lack of physical activity. He had been that star athlete in high school and continues to remain active – perhaps a little too much so. Paul is someone who obsessively works out. The kind of workout body builders do – the kind they call Open Chain Exercises (where weight is pushed or pulled but the body fixed and unmoving) and bilateral (where both limbs are used in unison to move the weight). His workout consists of the following: Monday chest and triceps, Tuesday back and biceps, Wednesday off (just some spinning), Thursday chest and triceps, Friday back and biceps, Saturday legs and cardio, and Sunday off.

Little ailments from his high-school football days have morphed into major pains – chronic shoulder pain, lower back pain, and knee pain. He is a thirty-two-year-old with the mobility of someone twenty years his senior. Although his physique is impressive, because of his pain he has difficulty performing the most basic everyday activities. Ironically, he has no trouble with bench presses or bicep curls. Why someone would want to be effective in the gym but ineffective in life escapes me. There is a limit one can achieve in physical activity – human strength, size, and performance have upper bounds but the downside effects are limitless (actually, there is a lower bound – death). Paul knows this but he continues his bad behavior.

He complains about all of his ailments like I had never heard them before. He does not like to hear it but I tell him what the probable causes of his pain are. It is a kind of a recursive game that work friends play – advice is asked, advice is given, advice is not heeded, repeat.

I tell Paul that he works out like he was a machine. Paul takes this as a compliment but it was not meant as one. You see, Paul – like most people –thinks of the human being as a machine. To the causal observer it would be a logical step. We are linear like machines – input A effects output B. A car might take 10 gallons of gas. On those 10 gallons, one might drive 150 miles plus or minus the number of miles due to external factors (e.g., low tire pressure). This is true of all cars. All in all, it is all very linear. So if we apply the same thinking for the humans – eat 1,000 calories and expend 1,500 calories through exercise and basal metabolism – we would eventually lose weight. But this is not the case.

There are people who consume more calories then they expend and do not gain a pound. Conversely, there are those who consume fewer calories then they expend but manage to gain weight. Input A may have no impact on output B (or the impact is random). So clearly, we are not linear beings and not machines. We are vastly more complicated, yet mainstream thinking has yet to catch up. I tell Paul he needs to stop training like a machine and to move more like a human. I quickly lose his attention. Back to work....

Suggested Reading/Resources

"Classics of Western Literature: Bloom County 1986-1989"

BY BERKE BREATHED

One of a number of books in this series but this one is *Bloom County's* best (for those unaware, *Bloom County* is a cartoon). After reading this, you will see that politics and the standard American lifestyle and satire have not changed much in the last 25 years. Opus may have even morphed into Bill Maher. The resemblance is striking.

Stretching Scientifically: A Guide to Flexibility Training

BY THOMAS KURZ

www.stadion.com

One of the first books that publicized the benefits of dynamic stretching and potential harm of static stretching prior to physical activity. The website is full of free articles on training, stretching and injury prevention, diagnostics, and treatment. Membership is free and there is a periodic newsletter and blog posting. Sister site www.real-self-defense.comcontains free articles on practical self-defense. They also sell the Unbreakable Umbrella. One note of caution, Tom Kurz is notorious for his curt and blunt answers to questions – so phrase your inquiries to him carefully.

Elastic Steel Method of Athletic Conditioning

www.elasticsteel.net

There is not a lot of free content but for purchase, the DVDs are well produced and informative, and cover a range of topics from martial arts to yoga. Free beginner stretching videos can be found at http://www.elasticsteel.net/Articles.asp?ID=319. Sister site www.bodyweightculture.com contains good postings and free video content. Membership is free.

Arthur De Vany's Evolutionary Fitness

www.arthurdevany.com

There are tons of valuable content on a broad range of topics including interesting and provocative subjects such as Death by Exercise, Intermittent Fasting, and Uncertainty. Content is posted frequently (at least twice a week) and Art provides empirical support for many of his assertions. Archives are searchable. Membership is approximately $40 for an annual subscription. It is well worth it.

CHAPTER 4 - 10:10 AM – THE UPSIDE-DOWN MAP

"Torture numbers, and they'll confess to anything." -- Greg Easterbrook

I am a procrastinator by nature. Before getting down to work, I will surf the Internet. I am interested in comparing my home value to other homes in the area (I have a 30-year fixed and am looking for strategies to pay off before I am too old and feeble to enjoy life). I browse to a well known free home comparison site that I had read a lot about recently in a number of middlebrow periodicals. I put in my street address and click "find comparables and estimate value." The results are shocking.

The automated estimate of my home is skewed down by 40% from when I first purchased it in 2005. It seems like the site's smart estimator just applied a flat percentage to my home value from when I first purchased it. This rate seems to be derived from the national average which of course is silly. Each market is very different (types of buyers, local economy, etc.) and the home price variance can be considerable (from a few thousand for a home to tens of millions), that using a flat national percentage is foolish. It also seems that the details of my home are incorrect and the other comparable homes selected by the site are questionable. I cannot but help to think of the scene in Monty Python's *Life of Brian* where a centurion, looking for Brian, tells his men to search a house because that was one place they had not looked. A large number of guards enter the house and shortly thereafter, exit the house. The lead guard says to the centurion, "Found this spoon, sir." The centurion says, "Well done, Sergeant." I feel like this site found me a spoon.

The phone rings. I see on my caller ID that it is one of my clients – Simon Renzio. I have not spoken to Simon in a few months, which clearly breaks a rule of "The Trusted Advisor" that requires more frequent attention. But Simon neither considers me a trusted advisor nor will I ever consider him worthy of my advisement. Simon is a technology and operations VP at a diversified financial institution (diversified financial institution is another word for too big to fail). He is best characterized by his need to micro-manage and his indecisive nature – a *folie du doute* of sorts. He is someone who has let work inhabit his every thought even when not at work.

Our jobs, if we take them too seriously, can be like a malady of the body and the mind. It slowly goes undetected with only minimal symptoms until it is too late and, retrospectively, we wished we had lived our lives differently – more balanced – more sustainable. Simon is overweight and has every risk factor for a heart attack. I am surprised he has lasted this long. I hesitantly pick up the phone with an inkling of what is about to transpire.

Simon is clearly upset. He rambles on about a project we complet-ed for him six months ago. Some of the figures were not coming out as expected and he wants to know why. I explain to him again as I had twelve months ago – that the problem was not with the work we did. It was with the work we did not do. The work we had proposed we do. The work that had to be done prior to the work we did. The work that exposed the true complexity of the issue and the weakness of the simple approach. He abruptly puts me on hold. I am left listening to an instrumental of "We Built This City on Rock and Roll."

The problem with Simon and most people in the financial ser-vices industry is that they are rewarded for the immediate future and not the distant future. Given this short-term incentive model, everyone – and I mean everyone – from front office, to middle office, to back office employees – will do just enough to get recognized for their short-term accomplishments. This is usually at the sacrifice of longer term (typically more sustainable) goals. These goals address the complexities inherent in addressing root cause issues and take time and resources to properly remedy. They have huge payoffs but on an extended term horizon. It takes courage for someone in the industry to look down the road. Simon does not have this courage.

Simon believed that he could circumvent the real issue by layering rational and well-thought-out arguments on a false premise. In this case, performing analysis and reporting on data that were of unknown quality and integrity (we all suspected that the quality and integrity were poor but did not have enough empirical evidence at the time). Even if we did, this would not have influenced the decision. He was moving forward with the project come hell or high water. Simon was called out by an enemy of his in another cohort, but a peer who recognized this fallacy. Something I call the Data Quality Fallacy.

The cliché "Garbage in/Garbage out" is often used in the business world as a means to quickly describe data quality issues that can plague an institution. If the inputs are wrong, then clearly any conclusions derived from it, regardless of how well reasoned, would be incorrect. This is obvious. Yet what is not so obvious is that once information enters the institution, its lineage through the institution impacts the quality of the data. In other words, as information moves through an institution from one process to the next and from one data warehouse to the next, it is transformed, enriched, and standardized to have more meaning to the business user. The issue is that when it moves from point to point, errors occur that go undetected. It gets compounded as the number of data sources and the number of points the data pass through increases (these gates could be manual or automated).

Data aggregators who source information from many institutions (or from multiple subsidiaries) have even a greater challenge. They need to harmonize data from various structures. Many even go as far as to make assumptions about data definitions. If a data point is stated as simply country, does this mean domiciled country, or country one does business in? What if one has addresses in multiple countries?

Furthermore, if data are significantly outside the defined typical pattern (outlier), they are often removed from the data set to optimize the analysis process (fewer data improve processing time). The problem is that, depending on how the data are to be analyzed, the removal of outliers can have no impact or significant impact. For example, one may remove small dollar transactions from a population of transactions because in total they do not have a material impact. However, on a per account or customer basis, they may have materiality. So if one is analyzing all transactions, the smoothing has a positive effect. However, if analyzing customers and/or accounts, the smoothing distorts the analysis.

People seem to ignore these data-centric issues and are unwavering in the belief that the data used to support and drive models, reports, and/or "dashboards") are complete and accurate. (I hate this term "dashboard" because it leads one to believe that the information and measurement used in, say, a risk dashboard is somehow just as accurate and precise as those used in a car's dashboard).

I have seen this many times at some of the largest financial institutions in the world. Actuaries and other quants use incomplete and inaccurate data to drive their models, many knowing the integrity of the data is questionable. When asked why they continue to use these data, to my amazement, they say that there is nothing better to use. This reminds me of Nassim Taleb's example from *The Black Swan* of a pilot flying into an airport and using the map of another airport. The data quality fallacy adds an additional dimension that makes the analogy even the more disjointed. Not only is the pilot using the wrong map, but the map the pilot is using is also substantially incorrect.

Financial service regulators are the only ones who can drive an institution to address the data quality fallacy (usually as part of a public order to make an example of an institution). But the regulators are the wrong people to address this issue. They are part of the problem on two ends: being equally blind as the bankers and then using the data in their own publications such as industry benchmarks and statistics. More precisely, financial institutions are required to file numerous periodic risk reports to one or more regulators. These reports contain specific information about the institutions' solvency or risk exposure. As I stated earlier, they are often wrong. Nonetheless, the regulators use these reports for their analyses – analyses that they publish. These publications are consumed by a number of organizations (universities) and used in their own analyses. The error just propagates and no one begs questions – is the supporting data accurate and complete? It is a game of who can better delude themselves.

The data quality fallacy is a systemic problem and affects all domains. Consider the recent events in the area of climate change. Proponents of global warming have used complex math and statistics to make the point that the climate is negatively impacted by humans. But it was discovered, through email leaks, that some of data used to support these models were of questionable quality. One cannot have a serious conversation using analysis derived from questionable data. As Carl Sagan, the famous skeptic, suggested in *The Demon-Haunted World*, if there is a chain of argument, every link in the chain must work – not just most of them. Arguing from a perspective with a known broken link with full disclosure is silly. Arguing from a perspective with a known broken link without full disclosure is fraud.

Simon takes me off hold and continues his rant. Before I can say another word, he hangs up on me. He clearly was not happy with my input and I should have known that he just wanted closure. This call was his *coup de grace*. Now he must shift to damage control. But there is no need to worry for Simon. He will not lose his job. Worst case scenario, he will lose some Brownie points with some Empty Suits. My future is not as bright. You see, there is a vicious irony as a consultant on matters such as this. Although Simon was forewarned of the implications of choosing the short-term approach, the blame for his failure will rest squarely on my shoulders. But on the bright side, Simon will not be calling me anymore.

Suggested Reading/Resources

Fooled by Randomness: The Hidden Role of Chance in Life and in the Markets

BY NASSIM NICHOLAS TALEB

www.fooledbyrandomness.com

Fooled By Randomness (the prequel to Taleb's bestseller *The Black Swan*) offers a view on how luck (and lack thereof) affects our life. He also takes us on a number of thought tangents on topics such as different types of biases in our thinking and uncertainty's role in happiness. For a work of nonfiction, his nonacademic narrative style is addicting. Taleb's website is atypical in the organization of content (one needs to see it to fully understand what I mean). For those that have the time, searching for the nuggets of wisdom strewn within the site is a pleasure.

CHAPTER 5 - 11:59 AM – OPTIMIZING OUR NATURE

"Man is the only animal for whom his own existence is a problem which he has to solve." -- Erich Fromm

Paul pokes his head into my office and asks me to lunch. He is accompanied by Victor Goldman. Victor is part of our team. He is very tall – about six feet four inches – and looks like he could have been a basketball player. In actuality, he was an accomplished tennis player. He has a bald spot where his yarmulke sits. Victor is a few years my junior with a superior intellect. He is fiercely skeptical but not a nihilist given his strong religious convictions. He is a *Bizarro* counterpart of the "Yes" man. Not to say he is the opposite and says no to all things, but rather, Victor is a man who will say yes if the argument is sound.

I appreciate this quality. He always challenges my thoughts and assertions. This has saved me the embarrassment of public ridicule on more than one occasion. But this quality of his is not appreciated by all. It can be dangerous to the Empty Suit, particularly in client meetings when coupled with his second great quality – his reckless courage. Victor will always point out a fallacy regardless of the situation. He will ask questions so incessantly he might be confused with a three-year-old in the stage of the "whys?"

Victor's early years at the firm were marked by pure dedication and a relentless work ethic. Rumor has it he worked forty-eight hours straight without rest on a high-profile crisis engagement. It seems that he wanted to impress his bosses and client through sheer hard work. He believed that effort and reward were symmetrical. We had warned him otherwise but most people need to experience pain before heeding a danger sign – like the toddler who is drawn to the hot stove regardless of verbal warnings. Needless to say, Victor, like so many others, was burned. I believe he was told that he was one of the smartest and hardest working in the group, but not one of the most important.

Indeed, a humiliating kick in the crotch, but more significantly a quality life lesson if one detects the hidden message. You see, there are two paths one can choose from when faced with such an indignity. I am sure Victor's boss knew this – at minimum, he, like most people, recognized that there is at least one path. The majority will choose the path to work harder – even though it is clearly not the attribute of the most important. The very few, however, will instantly understand. In fact, I am shocked to see Victor in the office today. In the vein of Timothy Ferriss' blog, The 4-Hour Workweek, Victor usually can be found tending to his garden or doing odd jobs around his house on any given business day. The rain must have changed his plans.

We head down together to the main cafeteria. Rumor has it that they were going to make it into a gym for the employees but decided on a cafeteria instead. The cafeteria is like any other cafeteria. There is a seemingly endless array of tables and chairs. A fixings bar sits squarely in the middle of this arrangement with the typical foofa of condiments like sweet relish and Thousand Island dressing. Off to one side of the cafeteria is the food preparation and selection area with one entrance and one regress. Inside this keep is a salad bar with all the toppings and hot and cold meal stations. Today it is more crowded than usual either because of the rain or the sausage and pepper Monday special.

I do not know why I even come down to the cafeteria. It is the same disappointment every time. Yet I keep coming. My memory plays tricks on me and recalls a cafeteria experience much better than actuality. Like a gambler who thinks the next pull of the slot machine will be substantially different from the last.

Honestly, I desire all the food in this room but my head tells me otherwise. I do not eat the deli meat because I do not know exactly what I am eating. I suspect a mixture of different body parts from a thousand different animals ground up and blended with saw dust and other food thickeners. I do not eat the pizza because of the cheese. I do not eat the bread because just like deli meat, it is a compilation of food stuff, in this case whey, high fructose corn syrup, and soy lecithin. I do not eat the greens because some are irradiated and others are covered with pesticides and herbicides. I always get the same thing (at least for the last few weeks) – a fruit cup with pineapple and melon, a coconut water (the kind with just coconut water), and a banana. I must confess, however, that on more than one occasion, I have snarfed soft dinner rolls from the cafeteria like an old woman who packs food into her handbag at an "all you can eat" buffet. Bread is just so addictive.

I get in line to pay for my food. I always end up in a line with a cashier who is the slowest. I think it may be my poor perception of long lines. It can be applied to any line like a line of traffic. I always seem to be in the lane that is not moving. When I switch lanes, invariably, the new lane becomes the lane that does not move. If I do not switch lanes, my lane remains the slowest. This phenomenon also happens at the supermarket. I will be patiently waiting in a line when a new register opens up. I quickly switch lines but never end up first. It never fails that the person in front of me ends up taking so long (usually has to do with a dispute of mere pennies) that I would have been better off not switching lines in the first place.

Today the lines are long and deep – my line in particular. People have piles of the nastiest food on their trays. Their eyes are bigger than there stomachs. But who can blame them. Eating is so complex. Not the act of eating of course, but all the psychology and cultural components. I think about our human ancestors before the advent of farming and animal husbandry some 10,000 years ago, and I wonder how they felt about food. How did these Paleolithic people live and what did they eat?

As a child, I was always perplexed by the size of the prehistoric peoples. It is said that the average height of an ancient Imperial Roman male was about 5 feet 5 inches[4]. The average height of an American male today is about 5 feet 10 inches. We have evolved quite a bit, my childish mind would infer – 5 inches in approximately 2,000 years. In my naivety, I would extrapolate from ancient Rome back in history. I concluded that the average height of a Paleolithic man 10,000 years earlier would be less than 4 feet. Going even further back in time yielded a race of dwarfs. And what of their teeth? We have dentists and oral hygiene to save us from a mouthful of dentures. But in Paleolithic times, there were no dentists, no toothbrushes, no toothpaste, and certainly no fluoridated water. As a child I thought that no one could live past twenty. They surely would starve to death with a mouth of only gums.

This is not the case of course. We have not linearly gotten bigger over time. My flawed logic of youth failed to take into account an extraordinary event in human history called the agricultural revolution. Studies of fossils from our Paleolithic ancestors suggest that the average height of a male was approximately 5 feet 10 inches in 16,000 BC. If that is the case, then why did we shrink to 5 feet 5 inches in the Common Era?

Studies suggest that the shift to breads during the agricultural revolution created a vitamin and mineral deficiency in humans. The breads of yesteryear were not fortified with vitamins and minerals as they are today and meat of hunter-gatherers proved a better source of protein and fibers.[5] The empty nutrition of bread negatively affected growth and introduced a host of other issues, such as the nascence of modern diseases and, of course, tooth decay. Tooth decay is not only a symptom of malnutrition; it is directly correlated with the increase of fermentable carbohydrates in the diet. In other words, the more bread you eat, the more decay you will have. [6]

It is counterintuitive, but the hunter-gatherers, although stronger in body, either assimilated by adopting agriculture and animal husbandry or were slowly eliminated by the masses of farmers. Today, there are only a limited number of humans living the hunter-gatherer way. Common knowledge suggests that natural selection should favor the fittest – the strongest – which would be the hunter-gatherers.[7] But in fact, natural selection only favors organism that can replicate better (survive and reproduce), which in this case are the masses of sickly farmers.[8]

The question then is, are our lives better now or better when we were hunter-gatherers? Have our evolutionary and technological advancements improved our condition or not? Clearly things have improved since the time of the ancient Romans but what of the Paleolithic period? We need to start our analysis by examining our current condition.

To a large extent we are animals like our Paleolithic ancestors but more domesticated. Perhaps a good evaluation point is to compare our condition to that of other domesticated animals. So what domesticated animal condition do we most resemble – how are we similar and how are we different?

It is not a stretch to compare ourselves to animals living in the zoo. They are somewhat domesticated. Erwan Le Corre has coined the phrase Zoo Humans. I think he is off the mark with this classification. We are not like animals in the zoo; rather we are more like factory farm animals. Zoo animals do live in an artificial environment, but their diet and surroundings more closely resemble their wild natural state. Even the animals themselves are hard to distinguish, at least visually, from their natural counterparts. Their keepers are benign and generally look out for their well-being. They are treated as living animals – organic creatures – and at least are treated with a shed of dignity. They are just pseudodomesticated.

Factory farm animals, however, live a very different existence. They are animals that are wholly domesticated through deliberate artificial selection – engineered if you will. They have been decoupled from nature and are treated as machines. It is in this difference that we are more like factory farm animals than zoo animals. Consider the following comparison.

We eat the same food

The factory farm animal's diet consists of grains (primarily corn) and legumes (primarily soy beans). They even get a dose of meat byproduct in their feed. Some feed is fortified with the ground body parts of diseased animals (incidentally, that is how mad cow disease spread amongst cows – through the ingestion of ground diseased cow brains by living cows[9]). Very rarely do factory farm animals eat what they were designed to eat, which is grass and other greens. Similarly, modern humans eat mostly grains and legumes of the same kind. Soy and corn (and there derivatives) can be found in most processed foodstuff. Although our intake of meat and meat byproducts is much higher than that of factory farm animals, the meat is sourced from factory farm animals. So we are getting an indirect dose of grains and legumes through the consumption of factory farmed meat. Hardly our natural meat supply (if one believes human are designed to eat meat).

We live in similar sterile environments

Both factory farm animals and humans live in sterile environments. Not literally sterile but figuratively sterile – environments that diverge greatly from our natural states. Factory farm animals are packed into huge windowless warehouses with little room to move[10]. Imagine the Lexington Avenue express during rush hour and the dangerously crowded conditions in each subway car. Although our conditions are not like this 24/7, we live in a world so devoid of nature it merits the comparison. Examine an aerial photo of the United States. Most metropolitan areas are exclusively gray with only the hint of green. Worse even is the night photo – the earth is a light bulb.

We get the same diseases

Factory farm animals and humans are plagued by many similar ailments given our comparable diets and living conditions. Given that we share many of the same diseases, we also take the same antibiotics. The antibiotics prescribed to factory farm animals are not only given to the sick animals. They are also given to the healthy animals as a preventative measure and in such large doses and frequency, that many of the bacterial strains they were meant to destroy have become resistant.[11] This would not be too worrisome but for the fact that these bacterial and viral strains also afflict humans. Bird and swine flues originate in farm animals and cross over to infect the human population. Similarly, mad cow disease is an affliction amongst cows that spread to humans in tainted beef products[12].

We overeat when it is possible to overeat

Confined factory farm animals that are being fattened for the slaughter eat more calories then they expend. They can hardly move and the only activity they perform is eating. That is how they get fattened. Sedentary humans have the same result. With little movement we also will overeat and get fattened. When we are inactive (as is with most mammals) we eat more than we expend. This is an evolutionary survival response. Our system protects itself from the randomness of food availability and the effort required to hunt and gather food. In other words, stuff your face with food because you do not know when your next meal will be. This made sense in Paleolithic times but not so much in modern times. If the food is in your face, it is very difficult not to eat it[13].

We are measured on our ability to produce

Productivity in itself is not such a bad thing. One should not labor in vain so that it produces no results. But if the results are not worthy of the labor, then one should not labor. It is in this regard that modern humans and the factory farm animal are similar. In most cases, what is produced by the human is low value (at least usually to the one that produces it). The result of factory farm production is death to the animal and diseased and filthy meat to humans. Both humans and factory farm animals are also considered machines – with inputs and outputs that can be measured, quantified, and optimized. Chickens are measured by their ability to make eggs or meat. They are engineered as a species to be optimized for each – layers and broilers respectively. Dairy cows have been so engineered they look very little like their ancestors even from three hundred years ago. The average cow in the 1700s produced 1 gallon of milk per day. In 2010, with the help of powerful growth hormones and breeding, a cow can produce over 20 gallons per day[14]. Try to imagine the size of the udder on a cow that must produce this unnatural amount of milk. This production cycle literally kills the cow, which then literally becomes dog and cat food (or your burger)[15]. Optimization of factory farm animals encourages strength only in the area that they are optimized. All other areas suffer, like health – thus the need to medicate with antibiotics.

Similarly, humans are measured on our ability to produce. The foundation of unions in the 19th and 20th century was to protect workers from over-utilization. Today, there is an economic productivity index that measures the amount of goods and services that a worker produces. Why is this bad, you may ask? Because it forces workers to specialize and optimize with regard only for their output. Proper treatment of the worker hardly makes the list. It also gives the specialist a sense of false security. Specialists thrive when times are good, but their inability to adapt makes them susceptible when times are bad. In other words, if they lose their job, they remain unemployed.

So it would seem that we are like factory farm animals – probably more so than we would like to believe. We know its effect and our condition is a reflection of what we are doing to ourselves. Although marketers would like you to believe otherwise, there is no such thing as a happy cow. Perhaps our happiness is just a facade as well. Perhaps we need to live like we had 10,000 years ago.

But it is not so easy to live our true nature in our modern world. Our normative standards (at least in the Western World) are much different now. We not only have to consider food – but also fitness, work, and personal lifestyle. You can make small changes in your diet without a neighbor noticing. But imagine walking around in public on a hot summer's day without deodorant. You will offend more than one person for sure. It is unfortunate, but to align with our nature, one must live off the grid – which of course is not for everyone. What we ought to do then is a matter of individual choice, the choice on how far one will go with one's change, the choice between the cost and benefit of personal health and beyond health – economic, environment, human rights, family, community, and spirit.

Regardless of the path taken, what is clear is that we cannot successfully optimize our nature. For every one step forward in the name of optimization, we take two steps back from our nature. The net effect is that we are strong in a very few areas and fragile in all others. We are moving faster than evolution will allow. We need to therefore focus less on optimization. We must live as though we are free-ranging, adaptive humans, not humans eating unhealthy food in cafeterias like factory farms animals being fattened in a warehouse for the kill.

I finally get to pay for my food. Victor and Paul are waiting for me. Their lines were faster than mine. We scour the cafeteria for an empty table and find one in the far corner. We sit down. As I sit,

I cannot help but to feel my pants tight around my waist. I have lost fifteen pounds over the last few months but my trousers are still tight. I had well intentioned goals when I had them tailored - perhaps a bit too optimistic. My belt, too, is not lying. It remains on the first notch. I think all my weight loss has been in my face and neck. I look like a pear stuck with a pin.

Of course we do not talk about our weight with one another. What men do that? Victor talks about Global Warming and how proponents of it have failed to convince skeptics and have hurt the cause of positive environmental change. The simple message of yesteryear of living in a toxic free environment was very convincing and changed policy. Today in Los Angeles you can actually see the mountain ranges whereas in 1980, all that was visible was pea soup. The message of clean air, water and land appealed to the common person. The negative effects of pollution were all around you – one could see it, taste it, smell it and feel it. The argument has relocated from a sensory forum to a cerebral forum. Now one must believe that the climate is warming and that humans are causing it. This, of course, is very difficult to prove. This is also what happens when you let Empty Suits lead your cause.

Paul shifts the conversation to lighter matters. He talks about how he ate lunch with a client and the client's sidekick last week. They went to a rustic steakhouse and the three sat at a table for four. When the sidekick sat down, Paul inadvertently sat next to him. This positioned Paul at the head of the table (that is to say he positioned himself to sit between the two others). Immediately, the sidekick stood up and changed his seat so his boss would be positioned at the head. It could not have been more obvious. We laugh at how silly people are but know that this is not the exception.

Victor talks about a staff of his – a newbie who started a few months ago. This newbie was so eager to impress, that whatever task Victor gave to him to work on, the newbie would finish almost immediately. So much so, that Victor had to keep feeding him work, until at last he ran out of work to give. This was frustrating as you can imagine. A lesson was in order. The next time the newbie eagerly asked for work, Victor had him perform the most mind-numbing documentation task that was made exponentially more difficult by the diagrams Victor also wanted created. One week later, the newbie came back to Victor totally exhausted. He had not completed the task. He had hardly even made a dent. Victor explained to him that this project was given to him as busy work. He explained to the newbie that work is not like a sprint or even marathon. Rather, it is more like gardening. You plant seeds and they will grow with time and care. If the newbie kept up his current pace, he would burn out in just a few years. Take the time to work, but also take time to be idle (a somewhat difficult task as a consultant where one is supposedly measured by the amount of time worked).

We quickly finish our food and hasten our way back upstairs. We do not want to be noticed by the roaming Empty Suits in the cafeteria. They may want to probe us. We would prefer to get back to work rather than to spend a moment of our time in mindless conversation with their type. It can only lead to trouble.

Suggested Reading/Resources

Eating Animals

BY JONATHAN SAFRAN FOER

A moving account of the author's journey and discovery on what exactly we are eating and how it is produced.

The Selfish Gene

BY RICHARD DAWKINS

Dawkins presents a gene-centric view on evolution rather than an organism-centric view. He coins the term *meme* that provides a model that asserts the evolution of human ideas is similar to natural selection.

The Grain Damage

BY DOUGLAS GRAHAM

www.foodnsport.com

A short, concise book highlighting the damage grains have done to human health and the environment. Dr. Graham is a fruitarian and the creator of the 80/10/10 diet (80% fruit carbohydrates, 10% protein from fruit, and 10% fat from nuts or fruits). His website offers free content and links to his books and other products for purchase.

The Meatrix

www.themeatrix.com

Three-part spoof of *The Matrix* that aims to educate on the harms of factory farming. The films are humorous and creative satires that use pop culture and entertainment to educate viewers about the food they eat and where it comes from.

Chapter 6 - 1:27 PM – Danger Zone: Empty Suits

"No fool like an old fool" -- Multiple attributions

Most children are forced to read poems for literature class. I must have read hundreds upon hundreds of poems in my lifetime. Few remain retrievable in my conscious mind and are from the likes of Edgar Allan Poe and Samuel Taylor Coleridge. Generally, poems are of the kind as to be read, reflected, and forgotten. But there was one poem I read as a child that struck me as profound – even at such a young age. The poem is called "Richard Cory" and it was written by Edwin Arlington Robinson.

Whenever Richard Cory went down town,

We people on the pavement looked at him:

He was a gentleman from sole to crown,

Clean favored, and imperially slim.

And he was always quietly arrayed,

And he was always human when he talked;

But still he fluttered pulses when he said,

"Good-morning," and he glittered when he walked.

And he was rich, richer than a king,

And admirably schooled in every grace:

In fine, we thought that he was everything

To make us wish that we were in his place.

So on we worked, and waited for the light,

And went without the meat, and cursed the bread;

And Richard Cory, one calm summer night,

Went home and put a bullet through his head.

I have been somewhat haunted by this poem over the years – it stays with me as I grow older. The lingering is a reminder that certain matters are more important than others. Nothing taps into one's sense of pity like a story of a wealthy old man, dying and without family, wishing he had done things differently. I suspect this is the case for the old fool Cory, but in his case, he did not wait for natural causes to free him from his distress.

I receive an instant message from one of my bosses, Leonard Hardacotch. We are a matrixed organization so I report to every-one on important matters (e.g., client needs some stroking) and yet no one on trivial matters (e.g., my raise, bonus). Nonetheless, he wants me to bear his tattoo so I can do his bidding within his practice – his pyramid. Before our client meeting, I suppose he wants to have a quick briefing.

Leonard: Need you in my office asap

(me): On my way. What's up?

Leonard: lets $ < time preppin for the 3 (translated means "Let us spend a little time preparing for the 3 o'clock client meeting")

My boss Leonard is an Empty Suit of the highest order (herein, Empty Suit will be referred to simply as ES - pronounced "ass," plural "ass-iz"). He is most recognizable by his case of split personality. I often do not know who I am talking to. Perhaps he has a twin. The discussions with him in the morning are forgotten by afternoon. Not so much forgotten, just the order of events has changed and some of the facts are distorted – often in his favor. When I question him on his memory of things, he is so strong in his conviction that I think perhaps I was mistaken. I usually do not take these matters lightly, but when someone projects such confidence, it is hard to believe otherwise. But also, I think intrinsically, humans have a natural apprehension towards standing firm against the sociopath. Someone who is so disconnected is something we fear. This disconnection is hard to articulate and even harder to reconcile. Leonard often believes that the information I had provided him earlier in a day – information that he confirmed at the time to be new to him – can now, later in the day, be his discovery. He asserts with such confidence and conviction that this information was in fact not new to him but rather new to me, and that he had first informed me of this information instead of my informing him! A very curious distortion indeed and perhaps another symptom of the ES.

I stand outside Leonard's office. His door is closed, but through a pane of glass adjacent to the door, I peer in. He gestures me. I hesitate, knowing that I am about to walk into a deep place where the sun is silent (and conversely a place that is also extremely shallow and loud).

I walk into Leonard's office. He is wearing a headset and with a wave of his hands gestures me to sit down. I spend some time just sitting and listening to him on the phone. I wonder why he immediately summoned me to his office if he was not ready to see me. Perhaps he received this call in the time it took me to walk here.

Leonard's office and my office do not resemble one another in any way. His office has windows, for one. It also is about three hundred square feet and includes a couch. He has a whiteboard on one of the walls. It is interesting how everyone seems to have a whiteboard nowadays when in the past they were only in the domain of engineers and computer programmers. Leonard's whiteboard is covered with chevrons – undoubtedly the most complex shape he knows of.

Leonard is a tall man who is in his mid-forties but appears much older. His cheeks are permanently red and his body has a certain softness about it that can probably be only fully appreciated with his shirt off. There is a looseness of skin under his chin somewhat resembling the jowls of the late Ted Kennedy – perhaps not as severe, but well on its way. His bookshelves are neatly ordered with business management books – the kind that lay out a number of simple steps needed to reach greatness that were derived by studying the attributes of successful managers and leaders. On his desk are a number of happy family pictures and photos with friends (most at golf outings). Perhaps this is to remind him why he works so hard. More likely, however, it is just a façade – a sort of wishful thinking strategy that is often recommended in self-help books. If he is surrounded by enough happy photos of his family and friends, it will elicit positive thoughts, then it will surely become reality.

I cannot help but notice the roast beef wrap with cheese and shards of lettuce sitting in a plastic takeout container on this desk. It oozes some cream sauce – perhaps Thousand Island or ranch. The smell is not appetizing and fills the room – a mix of raw garlic and onion. As he talks on the phone, I take the moment of respite to ponder on what sits before me – the platonic ideal form of an ES.

ESs are nothing new. They have existed all throughout history mainly in the political and religious arena. It is not until recently, however, that they invaded the corporate and science worlds. I have come across many ESs in my life. If you have ever worked for a large corporation, whether you know it or not you have come across an ES. They are ubiquitous at large corporations. They exist in smaller numbers in smaller institutions. ESs are overarchingly male but that may be a symptom of the glass ceiling rather than some esteemed quality present only in women. ESs are empty because they lack something. They may be intrinsically lacking, they may choose intentionally to lack, or they may simply be absent-mindedly lacking. They are not invisible – ESs will let you know that they exist.

The rather curious thing is that, although they will let you know they exist, they will never acknowledge that they are ESs. They will always point to the other chap. I suspect that they cannot see their own situation. It is the exact opposite phenomenon of middle class unawareness where both the millionaires and the working poor believe they are part of the middle class.

So it should not come as any surprise that the ES lacks self-awareness and the awareness that he or she does not know everything that there is to know. They are a physical manifestation of illusory superiority from the Dunning Kruger effect. Psychologists David Dunning and Justin Kruger set out to test Charles Darwin's assertion that "ignorance more frequently begets confidence than does knowledge." They tested this hypothesis on human subjects consisting of Cornell undergraduates who were registered in various psychology courses. In a series of studies, they examined self-assessment of logical reasoning skills, grammatical skills, and humor. After being shown their test scores, the subjects were again asked to estimate their own rank, whereupon the competent group accurately estimated their rank, while the incompetent group still overestimated their own rank. [16]

As Dunning and Kruger noted across four studies, the authors found that participants scoring in the bottom quartile on tests of humor, grammar, and logic grossly overestimated their test performance and ability. Although test scores put them in the 12th percentile, they estimated themselves to be in the 62nd. Meanwhile, people with true knowledge tended to underestimate their relative competence. Roughly, participants who found tasks to be relatively easy erroneously assumed, to some extent, that the tasks must also be easy for others. The Dunner Kruger effect demonstrated that there is a cognitive bias in which unskilled people make poor decisions and reach erroneous conclusions, but their incompetence denies them the ability to realize their mistakes[17].

This alone makes ESs dangerous. But even more so when coupled with power – either directly by their position or indirectly from the relationship and bond with other ESs.

It is relatively easy to become an ES. You do not need great smarts (although many ESs are very intelligent according to the common measure utilized in most schools and universities). Mostly, you just need to subscribe to a life where family, true friends, erudition, and health are not important. An ES knowingly enters and accepts that this is the path. You must also learn how to golf, but do not confuse the logic – not all golfers are ESs, but all ESs are golfers. You cannot become an ES by accident.

There are a number of notions put forth that attempt to explain how ESs actually ascend in an institution. The Peter Principle proposes that in business people will get promoted to one level higher than their competency level. If they were still competent at that level, they would get promoted up again. So they stop one level above where they naturally belong. The Dilbert Principle proposes that people get promoted because they will do less damage to the business at the new promoted level than at the current level. This would hold true less in the business realm and more in the field of engineering. God forbid an ES is charged with quality control of an airplane.

I think the Peter's Principle and the Dilbert Principle have some efficacy. But the ES Principle that I propose is something far simpler. ESs get promoted because those in power are usually ESs as well. ESs protect their own (at least for a time). Moreover, ESs, given their illusory superiority, see no risk in promoting a subordinate ES – when in fact this is risky. The same traits that make one ES desirable for promotion make another ES equally desirable. So in a way one can choose to become an ES – in other words, just choose to exhibit the traits of an ES. Therefore, unlike with the Peter Principle and Dilbert Principle, one can choose to be promoted. This could be wrong of course, but I shutter at the thought that the ES trait is not a matter of choice, but instead, reflexive (that it is to say, I unconsciously favors close genetic relatives such that those who look like me, talk like me, act like me, are naturally attracted to one another).

ESs can be toxic to the normal person. So avoiding them should be a priority. The first thing in avoiding an ES is to recognize when you are in the presence of one. Many of the same qualifiers for how to become an ES can be used to identify them on the street, on a job interview, or in a meeting.

First, ESs are not stupid individuals (incompetent and ignorant in certain matters but not wholly stupid). They can be in fact exceedingly intelligent. This can be book smart and/or people smart. But it is this very intelligence that is the facade. The paradox is that intelligent people can be exceedingly blind to their own limits of knowledge. So in other words, we are all biased in what we think we know and what we think we do not know. ESs raise the bar – they significantly overestimate what they think they know and significantly underestimate what they think they do not know.

Second, ESs are able to verbally articulate their thoughts well. That is not to say the thoughts themselves are logical or harmonious. Rather, they have an uncanny ability to convey their thoughts verbally in a convincing manner – usually by story telling. These narrative fallacies are convincing because the true complexities are hidden, and the message is delivered in a way to connect to the individual. Some may argue that this is the sign of a skilled presenter; however, I think it is the mark of a snake oil salesman. By oversimplifying the problem and the solution, a false premise is created. This is the angst of many project teams who need to deliver on a salesman's promise. I suspect this is the cause of many project failures.

Finally, ESs always have an answer, even when they do not know the correct one. They will never answer that they do not know and will construct elaborate responses to guise this fact. Depending on the situation and the audience, they will either overgeneralize (typically when talking with clients or bosses) or verbally attack with insults (typically when talking with peers and subordinates).

So how do you spot the ES? Look for the guy (again, ESs are mostly men) who does the most talking, whose ideas have lots of logical holes, and whose ideas are cloaked in a story spoken with verbosity and charm. Next, challenge him with a well reasoned argument pointing to the weaknesses in his narrative. Be level and calm in your questioning – and even self-effacing. Play devil's advocate if you must. When he is challenged, how does he react? If he exhibits rage (or the containment of rage) he is an ES, as challenging his thoughts are an assault on him personally. But beware; take heed when exposing ESs on internal company matters. If a whistle blows in a forest and only ESs are there to hear it, does it make a sound? The silence is deafening except for the momentary sound of a boot kicking an ass and the slam of a door.

Avoiding becoming an ES is simply a choice. A choice that there are other pursuits of greater worth in life and that the sacrifice required to become an ES is too great. An ES's life is a very hollow life only fit for the educated ignorant.

But there are repercussions if you choose a different path. I was on the path to becoming an ES in my life as a consultant. One of the interesting observations I noted when I decided not to become an ES was that, although my performance metrics across all categories were improving year over year, my relative performance rating to my peers was degrading. One might argue that my peers' performance was improving as well, and since the rating is relative to this peer group, then my rating would degrade. This reasoning is nonsense and that of a human resources representative who is disconnected from reality; the performance metrics of my peers were similar to my own. This inverse correlation is more than a random coincidence or an attribution of increased performance of my peers. When it became clear that I would no longer pursue the ES, the ESs rated me differently. Remember, ESs promote ESs. They rarely promote someone of another kind unless it meets their needs. This also goes to show that no matter what an institution touts as its objective performance measurements, when ESs are in charge, the measures are in fact highly subjective.

Most ESs will be ESs for life. The only way an ES can escape is through total humiliation and time. The more senior the ES, the greater the humiliation required and the greater amount of time needed to fully atone for his mistakes. Humiliation rocks their egos, but if they choose this way it usually can put them on a path to enlightenment. (It is a choice because the humiliating act is a result of the choices made as an ES.) Consider the case of Jerry Levin, former CEO of Time Warner. He, along with Steve Case, presided over one of the worst ES deals in the history of modern business with the acquisition of Time Warner by AOL (Sandy Weil is not far behind with the merger of Citicorp and Travelers insurance). Jerry was further humiliated when the organization full of ESs, CNBC, ranked him the worst American CEO of all time.[18] Interestingly, CNBC has a short and distorted memory, as they touted the deal. But this is something expected of an organization full of ESs. You know an organization is an ES organization when it fails to recognize its own hypocrisy and has the hubris to convict a former member of the same thing it is guilty of. In early 2010,

Jerry made penance, taking full responsibility for the disaster.[19] He has even gone so far as to alter his lifestyle, becoming a vegan among other things. You always need to be wary of former ESs that make contrition, but there is no reason to believe they cannot change given the right circumstances.

But what about those ESs that never apologize for their deeds and continue being ESs? They seem to always land on their feet. Even in the most egregious cases they are given only a slap on the wrist. In most cases, they are given golden parachutes (remember ESs care for their own). At the highest level, most politicians are ESs as are most board members and C-level executives at large institutions.

I have mixed feelings about ESs. Should they be pitied or should they be reviled? I prefer the latter and have often thought about the proper way they should meet their end. To look for a proper and fitting end to an ES, we will look to cartoons. There is a lot of wisdom in certain cartoons and in today's world they act as our moral compass – perhaps modern day myths of sorts. There are exceptions of course. Some cartoons have been used for propaganda (think of WWII cartoons) and others reflect certain societal intolerances of the time (think *Sambo* cartoons). But I find that most cartoons contain nuggets of wisdom that can be gleaned from slapstick comedy and cultural misgivings.

My favorite is called *Chow Hound*. It is a Looney Tunes cartoon from the early 1950s. Up until 2001, this cartoon was uncut. But perhaps because of its very clear and explicit moral message it was cut to remove the last minute of the story. In short, the story is about a greedy bulldog who scams local residents out of money and steaks with the help of a cat and mouse, both of whom are held against their will and forced to act as mules. The bulldog treats the mouse, and particularly the cat, very poorly – often beating them after they pull off a scam – complaining, "What, no gravy!?!?" After successfully executing a number of scams, the bulldog earns enough money to purchase a meat deli with a seemingly endless warehouse of hanging meats.

The final scene occurs in a hospital. The bulldog lays motionless on an operating table, grossly obese from all the meat he has consumed. (For the Monty Python fan, the size of the bulldog and his state of sloth is similar to the morbidly obese Mr. Creosote before exploding over several restaurant patrons in *The Meaning of Life*.) Two visitors arrive – the cat and the mouse with a funnel and industrial-sized container of gravy. They insert the funnel into the bulldog's mouth as he sweats and cries, helpless on the table. The cat says, "This time, we didn't forget the gravy" as they begin to pour the gravy into the funnel and the scene fads out. Justice is a low-level quality and there are more noble qualities to pursue before justice. But justice is very satisfying and I will indulge myself. Ah yes, Chow Hound Retribution, a very fitting end for an ES.

Leonard abruptly ends his call, takes a bite of his wrap, and asks me to brief him on why we are having a meeting with the client later today. Before I can begin, he offers me a bite of his sandwich. A polite insincerity, I suppose, and I gently refuse. He looks at me as though I insulted him. He says, "Oh, I forgot, you are one of those." I suppose he associated my refusal with the fact that I do not eat meat – or dairy for that matter. I am a bit stunned and find it difficult to answer. What if it were against my religion? A very shallow man, Leonard is. I try to contain my disgust and contempt and seek solace in knowing that he is living the consequences of his choices. And although I am not one who forecasts, it is a simple extrapolation to see where his end is.

I smile and continue with the debrief. I try to keep the conversation high level as I do not want to confuse him with the details. I already know what Leonard will say. He distills all problems, issues, challenges, and opportunities down to three points – or in PowerPoint speak, three bullets. It is funny that all ESs choose this route – it's always three points. As if there were a school for ESs that teaches that three points is the perfect level of distillation – like a secret code amongst ESs.

These three points and what we build around them are what we are to tell the client. We will provide them comfort that the complexities are not complex at all. We can now easily back into the client's fee expectation. In other words, the client tells us the problem and gives us a sense of what he is willing to pay – this is usually much less than the fees needed to complete the job, given the complexities. So instead of helping the client understand this, which takes some courage, we reduce the complexity of the problem by deluding ourselves and then convince the client that our delusion is reality. Now the fees can easily be reconciled with the complexity.

He asks if I can pull a placemat together for our meeting. Placemats are common in the consulting world. Before consulting, the only time I came across a placemat was at a restaurant or at a child's play table. But in consulting, it is all about simplicity, or more accurately, masking complexity. His request, though, is a Catch-22 – if I say I cannot, given that I only have about an hour to do it, this will go into my performance review under "fails to plan effectively." If I say yes, I reset the expectation bar for the next time he makes such an absurd request.

So I am off to pull a quick placemat together highlighting his three points. I will also construct a framework around it to demonstrate how smart we are. A few diagrams will add the "wow" factor. I want to do a good job and win the work because that is what I do. That is what I am measured against. That is how I am validated. But I know better and secretly wish we lose. I know that delivering on the promises will be next to impossible and that the team responsible for delivering will most likely suffer. Suffer through working twelve-hour days. Suffer through working weekends and holidays. Suffer by facing the insults from Leonard and the client on their incompetence. Suffer from the performance review that will evidence the contrived incompetence with no mention of the failure on the sales team for selling an unattainable expectation. And so I prepare.

Suggested Reading/Resources

Throwing the Elephant: Zen and the Art of Managing Up

BY STANLEY BING

What Stanley calls Elephants, I call Empty Suits. Regardless, this short book is humorous and offers tips on how to handle one – especially if the Elephant wearing the Empty Suit is your boss.

The Anosognosic's Dilemma: Something's Wrong but You'll Never Know What It Is (Part 1)

BY ERROL MORRIS

First article in a series of four published in the *New York Times* on the Dunning Kruger Effect. The first part is a must-read and hilarious to say the least. It can be found at http://opiniona-tor. blogs.nytimes.com/2010/06/20/the-anosognosics-dilemma-1/

Chapter 7 - 2:22 PM – The "Stone Soup" Aside

"Every sin is the result of a collaboration" -- Seneca

I am back in my office. What is the best way to pull this placemat together? It is very hard to build something from scratch. I think that is why there is so much plagiarism. It is easier to improvise from a base of work than to create from a blank slate. This is an important aspect of business to know as it relates to all kinds of intellectual property.

But the most important aspect of business that I know I learned from a software game published in the early 1980s by the name of M.U.L.E (Multiple Use Labor Element). What a great game it was. You and three other players compete for various limited resources (Food, Energy, Smithore and Crystite) on your newly colonized world – planet IRATA (that is Atari backwards – how clever).

Aside from the entertainment it provided, the aspect of the game that, when executed correctly, always tilted the odds of winning in your favor was collusion. You effectively could hoard resources, set artificially high prices, and crush your opponents slowly. I remember clearly the calls of unfairness and fits of crying from all the sore losers – it was the hallmark of every game. The concept of collusion has stuck with me outside the world of games. It is something inherent in real life in all kinds of business. There are even laws enacted to curb collusion, but it is so monetarily advantageous that people continue to find ways to pull it off (think about all of the insider trading that goes undetected). One way to benefit from collusion while playing by the rules is to use its guised positive form – collaboration.

I pull out an old PowerPoint presentation that I created previously with the help of about ten other individuals. Typically, if I need to pull a presentation together and I have some time (a couple of days at least), I leverage something I call the Stone Soup method of presentation development. I believe this is the same process the open source community uses to develop their various shareware. It is very effective. Just look at Wikipedia.

First, let me ramble a bit on the genesis of the method. The Stone Soup method is based on the lessons from an old folk tale about two soldiers returning home from a war in Eastern Europe (the tale has many slight variations but this is the gist of it). They carry nothing but an empty pot. As they return home, they grow hungry walking through the countryside. They happen upon a village that appears to be deserted. But it is not, as many of the villagers have hidden themselves inside their homes upon seeing the two strangers approaching. The two soldiers are very hungry and proceed to go from home to home looking for food. No one answers. They know the village is inhabited and they suspect that the villagers do not want to share their food stores with them. The two soldiers decide upon a plan.

They go to the village square and set up their large pot and fill it with water. They start a fire, boil the water, and throw into it a large stone. Curious, a villager peers out his window. His curiosity helps him summon the courage and he leaves his home to investigate what exactly the two soldiers are up to. He approaches them and asks what they are doing. They reply that they are cooking stone soup. One of the soldiers tastes the soup with a spoon and with a curious look on his face, insists that it is almost perfect. It just needs a little meat. The villager replies that he has a small amount of spare meat and he would be happy to share. The villager quickly goes to retrieve it and soon returns and supplies the soldiers with the meat. They quickly add it to the soup. More and more villagers become curious and approach the soldiers. As each villager approaches, one of the soldiers tastes the soup and replies that it is almost perfect except that it is missing a small amount of one ingredient or another. Each villager agrees to share the little that they have and retrieves a small amount of the missing ingredient. One after another, each villager contributes an ingredient to the soup. The soup eventually morphs from boiling water with a stone to a thick and hearty soup.

I have used the lessons of cooperation and collaboration from this story in the development of many of PowerPoint presentations. Most people have in their computer files one or more PowerPoint presentations of varying levels of sophistication and quality. These are typically coveted by those that possess them. Within each presentation, there are usually one or two slides that are very unique. In the business world, it is less about what you know and more about what you have (in this case, what you have saved from current and former employers).

Given that it is difficult to create something from nothing, convincing others to provide these nuggets is critical. Critical at least until you have amassed your own collection of presentations. We will assume that there are three types of people that we are targeting: 1) those that will never share, unless they are peer-pressured into it, 2) those that will share openly as long as asked, and 3) those that will share only if they receive some benefit.

The following method will work on all three personality types. Start by sending an email to the individuals that you know are hoarding a treasure trove of presentations, and ask if they can assist with the development of the presentation (be sure to use the words "we" and "our" and not "my" or "mine.") There should be one ringer in the email population – the second soldier who knows what you are up to. Provide in the email as an attachment an outlined and sparsely populated PowerPoint presentation. Ensure that some important bosses are cc'ed on the email and send. If you do not receive a response shortly thereafter, send an updated email with an updated PowerPoint presentation with some slides rearranged and the addition of one slide (this should be a slide that looks valuable).

Let everyone know that the process is coming along well and thank everyone, especially soldier 2, for the contributions so far. This will be the catalyst for people to begin providing their treasures. The first person to provide will be someone from person type 2 category. (They may even respond before the second email is sent. If that is the case, thank them as well in the update email). Feeling that they have something to share and warrant some credit, someone from the person type 3 category will begin providing their wares. They will probably reply with an attachment along with a very verbose email with lots of puffery. Ignore it – all you care about is the attachment.

The presentations will start flooding in as one person will try to outdo the other. Finally, someone from the person type 1 category will provide something. What they have to share is usually the Queen's Crown. They have no choice but to share because they will appear not to be team players if they do not. No one can afford that in the business world, particularly when important bosses are aware. Before you know it, you will have enough content to draft something truly unique and of high quality. And you will also receive kudos from your bosses. They will commend you on your team skills as much as they will on your presentation. Particularly if they are ESs – they often confuse movement for action.

But beware. If you share the final version with the group, there may be the one sycophant that will try to take all the credit. He or she will be the one who immediately, after you send the final version, responds with an email noting that they made some minor modifications to your presentation when in fact they just replied with the same attachment and did nothing of the sort. This is the email the bosses will actually look at. But alas, you should not care. You were able to create Stone Soup – and save yourself tons of time in the process. That is all that really matters.

I open up some old presentations and do a quick copy and paste job into a placemat format. I make some minor modifications to the client name and team members attending. Everything else more or less falls into place. I send it off to reproduction to make hard copies for the meeting.

Suggested Reading/Resources

The 4-Hour Workweek: Escape 9-5, Live Anywhere, and Join the New Rich

BY TIMOTHY FERRISS

Offers some practical and impractical tips and tricks on how to make the most amount of money for the least amount of work. The trick on becoming a top expert in four weeks is an interesting one. This may explain the expert problem (see Suggested Read-ing/Resources in Chapter 2). Seriously, though, the book is a unique take on being a successful slacker. I do not, however, understand the quote dropping and relevance in each chapter and subchapter – they seem to be randomly placed. But perhaps mine are no better.

Chapter 8 - 3:00 PM – Logic is in the Eye of the Beholder

"Any man can make mistakes, but only an idiot persists in his error." -- Marcus Tullius Cicero

I never put much confidence in the outcome from a sales meeting (orals as they are called in the consulting world) or from sales efforts in general. I have found that there is no predictable correlation between my skills or my colleague's skills and whether or not we win or lose a sales opportunity. It is completely random (of the kind of randomness where I do not have all the available information but someone controls the outcome). When I think we will win with a stellar proposal and the inside scoop, we lose. Conversely, in the cases where I am sure we will lose, such as when our fees are grossly inflated and we have no relationship with the client, we end up winning. This does not bother me so much anymore as I have come to accept this complete uncertainty. It is how my bosses view this matter that I struggle with.

They believe that when we win, it is due to something intrinsic in our knowledge of the problem or our trusted advisor relationship with the client – even though when both of these are true, we often lose. And when we lose, they believe it is a failure of our team, either the failure to draft a stellar proposal or the failure to establish an emotional bond with the client. Again, even when both of these are true, we often win. They never seem to recognize it, and if they do, they do not acknowledge it. This may just be another symptom of an ES – unconditional belief that there are known and purposive patterns for everything.

Leonard and I meet in the office lobby. We are greeted by Ron Myers. Ron is the business development executive for the account. In other words, he is the official salesman for this client. Ron is in his mid-forties and is noticeably gray. Although I have met Ron hundreds of times before, he still does not remember my name. His memory is not at fault as he has a knack of always remembering client names. He just does not consider me important enough to waste memory space.

We proceed outside. Ron mentions that if we do not catch a cab, we will have to dial into the call. Leonard agrees. This might be true if there was not a bus or a subway we could take to get to the client. I will err on the side of caution with these two fellows and assume that they are just too highbrow for those modes of travel rather than exceedingly stupid (we are in Manhattan – there is a bus stop and subway station on every corner). Taking positions on separate corners, we all attempt to hail a cab. Given the rain, it takes us upwards of ten minutes to finally catch one. I enter the cab first, followed by Ron. Leonard ventures into the street and enters the cab from the opposite door which effectively sandwiches me between the two and forces me to take the middle seat. I sit crumpled with my work bag on my lap and with my legs uncomfortably perched atop the awkward hump that separates the left seat from right.

As we are making our way downtown, there is the uncomfortable silence among us. Ron breaks the silence and asks if there will be any "skirts" or "BLs" at the meeting. He failed to ask ahead of time and is concerned that we may not look diversified. Leonard laughs and says that there will not be any attending, at least none that he is aware of. Why, he says, would the client want to dumb down the meeting? He and Ron chuckle.

I just sit in silence. I suppose "skirt" is better than saying "bitch" and "BL" is better than saying "nigger." And Leonard was only joking about the dumb-down bit. Perhaps I am too sensitive. Even my mental excuses cannot convince me that this vileness is pleasant. I am uncomfortable but feel helpless. How does one respond in such a situation? Should I say something, and if I do, what am I aiming to do – educate or reprimand? It is not in my nature to stir the pot, so I just sit there – emotionless, as if I had not heard anything. But I do not feel good about my impotence.

We arrive at the client and spend a quarter of an hour checking in at security. We are in the book (that is the list of people that can enter) but security is holding us up because they cannot reach our contact. Eventually they just let us through for no apparent reason other than we are in the book. We hustle to the elevator and take it to the 28th floor. We squeeze our way on. The door closes. "I Shot the Sherriff" instrumental is gently playing from the invisible elevator speakers. Instrumentals of popular music sound so odd. I suppose people make a living doing it or it would not be so popular on elevators (or when on hold during phone calls). We stare at the numbers that are above the elevator door. They illuminate as we pass each floor but just a haphazard flicker. The elevator rises quickly and my ears pop. We arrive at the 28th floor.

We are the only ones to exit the elevator at 28. We are trapped in the elevator bank because we do not have a security badge to buzz ourselves through the door. After we knock on the door for a time, someone kindly opens it for us. They look at us with suspicious eyes as I suppose they know they have violated some security policy by letting us in without a badge. We head over to the main reception area where we randomly meet one of the client's proxies. They are shocked to see us, but then quickly change their tone. They must have forgotten that we have a meeting scheduled. They escort us to a corner conference room – a holding pen for now.

The room is gray and cold with wall-to-wall windows. The view is picturesque but we have limited visibility due to the rain and fog at this height. We fumble to turn on the lights like a man fumbles with a fuse box during a blackout (these new conference rooms have a number of unmarked switches and buttons). When the lights are finally turned on, the florescent transforms the room from gray to ice. We take random seats at the large conference table (It may not be so random. I am sure Leonard and Ray have some method). Slowly, the client's team begins entering the room. We exchange polite insincerities, and as a good consultant I fumble in my pocket for my business card.

I always feel uncomfortable with the ritual of business card distribution. I cannot pinpoint exactly why, but I think it may have to do with feeling presumptuous. Presumptuous that after this meeting, they would actually want to contact me based on what we discussed. Perhaps I would be more comfortable with providing my card after the meeting upon request. Nonetheless, I feel peer-pressured by Leonard and Ron who instinctively begin passing out their cards. As we do this, most, of course, do not reciprocate. They know better (in other words, once a consultant gets your card, you are forever in their Rolodex). On the other hand, I am sure my card will be quickly tossed away when the meeting is over.

One of the client's proxies (a sycophant for sure) does provide us with his card. He hands it to me. It reads his name with a series of acronyms CIA, CISA, CITP, PMP, CPA, CFE, IFRS... This is a clear giveaway that this individual is an ES in training. This individual believes that these acronyms (and the credentials they imply) qualify him as one who possesses a deep knowledge of his trade. Like a doctor, who after years of training and study, provides his credentials of MD. However, in the business world, no acronym – not even the highly coveted MBA – should be on one's business card. It screams the opposite of the professional. Business card acronyms are the anti-aphorism. They are sound bites of either the oblivious (such as, you are unable to put yourself in my shoes, because if you could, you would see the ridiculousness of it) or the incompetent narcissists (such as, you need to mask your incompetence with these acronyms and hope no one calls you out on it).

I take the placemats out of my bag and hand them to Ron. He begins passing them out. The Client enters. He appears to be grumpy – clearly he had forgotten about this meeting and we interrupted some quality Internet surfing. He sits down, pulls out his BlackBerry, and begins typing something. Arrogance wafts from him like the smell of cheap cologne from a gigolo.

One of the client's team members dials into a conference line (one of the starfish phones that are ubiquitous in conference rooms). A number of people beep in and then introduce themselves. I suspect they will all go on mute notwithstanding the one listener who will put his line on hold and the meeting will be interrupted with the sounds of elevator music.

The Client returns to the present from his BlackBerry world. He says half jokingly, "What are we waiting for, let's get this over with." So we get down to business. Leonard begins walking the client through our placemat. It is a very lively conversation with a lot of verbal parlances between Leonard, the Client and his proxies. Ron interjects at certain points like all salesmen do with random non sequiturs that kill the verbal flow. I am unsure what his strategy is but, since most salesmen are clueless of the business problem, I suspect Ron is just trying to sound smart and relevant. In spite of the interruptions, Leonard, the Client and the client's proxies smoothly continue on and seem to take great pride and joy in their verbal joust. I just sit and listen as they go back and forth. Their logic flows like a Monty Python movie. I cannot help but just listen and grin.

Leonard: There are ways of telling whether she is a witch.

Proxy 1: Are there? Oh well, tell us.

Leonard: Tell me. What do you do with witches?

Proxy 1: Burn them.

Leonard: And what do you burn, apart from witches?

Proxy 1: More witches.

Proxy 2: Wood.

Leonard: Good. Now, why do witches burn?

Proxy 2: ...because they're made of... wood?

Leonard: Good. So how do you tell whether she is made of wood?

Proxy 1: Build a bridge out of her.

Leonard: But can you not also build bridges out of stone?

Proxy 1: Oh yeah.

Leonard: Does wood sink in water?

Proxy 1: No, no, it floats!... It floats! Throw her into the pond!

Leonard: No, no. What else floats in water?

Proxy 1: Bread.

Proxy 2: Apples.

Proxy 3: Very small rocks.

Proxy 1: Cider.

Proxy 2: Gravy.

Proxy 3: Cherries.

Proxy 1: Mud.

Proxy 2: Churches.

Proxy 3: Lead! Lead!

Client: A Duck.

Proxy 1: If she weighed the same as a duck... she's made of wood.

Leonard: And therefore...

Proxy 2: ...A witch!

In the consulting world, a good listener can be mistaken for someone who knows nothing. However, when in a room filled with ESs and their sycophants (and the oddball salesperson), one is best served to remain quiet. Together with some gently nodding, one can cruise through the verbal mess without saying a word. It is at moments like this when an interjection from a junior staff would help shake things up. They are too green to know that they are not supposed to speak or, in the case of Victor, they just cannot control themselves when others spew such blatant fallacies. But alas, there is neither Victor nor a junior staff present today.

The logic that was parlayed was riddled with fallacies. It was hard to keep from cringing. The casual observer might think these gentlemen are exceedingly stupid. But in fact, all of them hold degrees from accredited universities. So what is going on? How can someone intelligent by the common measure spew such blithe ignorance?

The answer lies in rhetoric. They have chosen to use rhetoric rather than good reason to make their case. Rhetoric does not need to be either logical or fully accurate — it just needs to be convincing. Historically, its place and influence are in politics and religion. It has swayed people against the better good and common sense. Juvenal lamented over the Roman zeitgeist of bread and circus and Marx observed that religion was like an opiate for the masses.

But in recent times, rhetoric has infected business and science – so much so, it is hard to discern the truth. For example, we all know that $2 + 2 = 4$. But in the rhetoric of pharmaceutical science, $2 + 2$ can equal 8 when a drug study convincingly finds a drug doubles the effect of the output. In the rhetoric of finance, $2 + 2 = 0$ because the credit risk in the expression can be transferred to investors. Rhetoric just does not add up.

Rhetoric relies on point of view and that is the root of the issue. When we introduce point of view as the axiom, then the truth is beholden to the individual (or cohort). There is an advertising effort that illustrates the problem of point of view. A global diversified financial institution commissioned a number of ads called "Different Values." In each one, a single image repeats three times, with a different one-word interpretation imposed over each photo. The one that struck my attention is called "Shaved Head." The words "style," "soldier," and "survivor" overlay the photo of the back of a gender-neutral shaved head. The fourth panel reads the tag line, "Different values make the world a richer place." This tag line holds true for certain things, like a rug or a piece of chocolate. But in other areas there are absolute and objective truths – no gray areas. It either is or it is not. What if the advertisement showed emaciated Jewish prisoners in Dachau and tagged it "Hungry," "Conspiracy," "Holocaust." Do different values really make the world a richer place?

With rhetoric, truth becomes gray and allows individuals to interpret as they like – sloth becomes leisure, envy becomes respect, lust becomes intimacy, avarice becomes ambition, gluttony becomes good health, wrath becomes justice, pride becomes personal worth, and vanity becomes positive self-image. Rhetoric allows Dick Fuld, former CEO of Lehman Bank, to sit before Congress unapologetic for his actions even though Lehman hid billions of dollars of risk exposure to the public and ruined thousands of lives.[20] It allows Merck to release Vioxx knowing that its controlled studies were empirically weak and the drug was unsafe.[21] It allows Monsanto to create genetically modified seeds that do not reproduce so it can corner the market. Rhetoric allows 90% of all published medical studies to be exaggerated, misleading, or flat-out wrong. [22] Do not let anyone fool you; there is an objective truth in certain matters. When it is left to rhetoricians and individual point of view, disaster soon follows.

The Client is clearly pleased with the conversation and the value proposition. This one seems like it is in the bag, which I suppose was the objective of the meeting. I find it all very frustrating as this all goes against every grain of my being. I do not subscribe to this rhetoric. I feel no emotion but my mind struggles to reconcile my reality with my reason. I am fatigued by this exchange because it is so wrong.

Suggested Reading/Resources

The Black Swan: The Impact of the Highly Improbable

BY NASSIM NICHOLAS TALEB

www.fooledbyrandomness.com

Very convincing ideas on uncertainty among others including our inability to correctly forecast, identify correct patterns, and predict the right reason for past events. He uses clever analogies and words of his own making to further argue his points. Tons of bite-size information in the postscript. Similar to *Fooled by Randomness*, his nonacademic narrative style is addicting. Taleb's website is atypical in the organization of content (one needs to see it to fully understand what I mean). For those that have the time, searching for the nuggets of wisdom strewn within the site is a pleasure.

The Stoic Philosophy of Seneca: Essays and Letters

TRANSLATED BY MOSES HADAS

Selected essays and letters from the Roman Stoic philosopher
Seneca. He tutored and advised Nero before being forced to com-
mit suicide. His works are one of a handful on Stoic philosophy
that still exist today. His letters and essays are portioned into bit-
sized nuggets of wisdom and are easily digestible.

**Thank You for Arguing: What Aristotle, Lincoln, and Homer
Simpson Can Teach Us About the Art of Persuasion**

BY JAY HEINRICHS

Humorous and informative book on the art of persuasion.
Provides strategies, tips, and tricks on how to persuade and how to
recognize when being persuaded.

Skeptic Magazine

www.skeptic.com

Official website of the Skeptics Society founded by Michael
Shermer. Contains tons of free articles from the weekly *eSkeptic* newsletter among other free and for-purchase products. The
quarterly *Skeptic Magazine* publication requires a subscription. This
also automatically enrolls you as a member of the Skeptics Society.
Now that's cool.

CHAPTER 9 - 4:45 PM — NEGATIVE POWER OF POSITIVE THINKING

"It is a habit of mankind to entrust to careless hope what they long for, and to use sovereign reason to thrust aside what they do not desire." – Thucydide

I arrive back in my office from the client meeting. I collapse into my chair. Leonard and Ron said they felt good about this one and were sure that the Client was impressed. Ron was so sure in fact, that he was going to book this one in the system. Ron must be very confident indeed. Booking in the system means that one is accountable for the outcome. As you can imagine, most opportunities are booked after they are won.

I am exhausted. I feel flush and make my way to the men's bathroom. I hurry to the sink and douse my face with some cool water. I notice in the mirror that I have broken out with a rash – perhaps hives. This is something that it not new to me. It has happened before but is something that has only affected me in my adult life. I am not positively certain what is the cause given the infinite number of possibilities but stress seems to be at minimum a component. The frequency of occurrences has increased in recent years as I learn more about how the world really operates. I return to my office.

I get an instant message from a buddy of mine – Jan Cosmescu (we like call him John for gender clarification reasons). John emigrated from Romania and is a fifteen-year veteran with the firm. When I first met John, he was dressed in an athletic suit and was wearing one of those pepino hats that also are known as newsboy, ivy, driving, sixpence, and scally caps. This type of cap is ubiquitous in Eastern Europe. John also has a thick Romanian accent that for the untrained ear, one would assume to be Russian. I hastily generalized that he was either a gangster or elite chess player. He was neither, but coincidently he is a Mensa member – but of the kind that is profoundly humble and not condescending in any manner.

He has had a recent run of bad luck losing both his mother to a sudden aneurism and his wife to the charm of a young attorney. John is also behind on many of his performance targets this year. He has not been selling like he used to. I suspect it is just a streak of bad luck related to his personal losses and will normalize over the year. He has been hoping that things will change.

John: Hey skippy. What's going on????

(me): Just got back from a client meeting. Got a serious headache. What's up

John: What happened?

(me): Typical meeting - don't want to get into details but same old stuff

John: Sorry to hear dude.

(me): Its ok, whats up?

John: I wanted to know if you had client contacts we can use as quals. Need it for a proposal

(me): Sure - will send them to you. But need to first get their permission. Will keep you posted

John: Ok - but proposal is due in two days. Maybe we submit the names and ask the client not to contact until we confirm

(me): Sure - then I'll just send them to you

John: Thanks - this is a good one

(me): What do you mean??

John: If I win this, I'll be set for the year

(me): Nice - who is the client?

John: Acme Capital Management

(me): You know about them right

John: Yeah, but I met with the COO and have a good feeling about it

(me): Nice

John: ok, gotta run, ttyl

(me): ltr

I am afraid this new opportunity at Acme will not bode any better for John than any of his previous failed opportunities. You see, Acme Capital Management is notorious for using our proposals to gauge the value of their preferred provider. This has always been the case for Acme. Unless something has materially changed (which I am not aware of but of course could be true), he is just wasting his time. John is supremely intelligent but even he is not immune to the biases of positive thinking. The fact that "he feels good about it" makes me feel uncomfortable about it. We like to think we can "will" an event to happen. I suppose it is a place of comfort with all the uncertainty in our lives. But alas, we cannot simply hope that an event occurs. Most events in modern life are not in our control and the few that are require more than simply hope. John will lose this work and will suffer all the negatives that come along with it. I hope I am wrong.

John's positive thinking fallacy is not anything new to me. There are three kinds of positive thinking in organizations that collectively form the Corporate Positive Thinking Fallacy: 1) Positive thinking from misleading managers (also known as drinking the Kool-Aid, which I suppose is an offhand reference to the Jonestown Massacre), 2) positive thinking arguments from wishful peers (like John), and 3) positive thinking from deluded subordinates.

I see the latter every day in one form or another manifested in one subordinate or another. Take the following for example; I am a mentor to a number of junior staff. The delusion among many of the newest hires is astounding. I am not talking about the typical delusion of youth such as how they truly believe they can change the world. I am sure a handful will, but that is small in comparison to all of those who try. The delusion of this new generation is the grand expectation of top salary and position with no experience. It is as if they believe that the knowledge and wisdom gained from a long and experienced lifetime is in their possession by simply graduating from university. It may be rooted in the "everyone is a winner" mentality instilled in them by their parents and teachers. There was a time when there were clear winners and losers. Today, everyone is a winner – even the ones that are clearly the losers. Trophies and first place blue ribbons for all. This approach to life is neither realistic nor fair. It does not prepare our children for the real world where there are clear winners and losers. They will have little capability to manage life's many disappointments.

This belief presents itself at year end when performance is evaluated and decisions on promotions, raises, and bonuses are published. My mentees cannot fathom when decisions are not in their favor. What is it, I ask them, that supports your argument for a promotion, raise, or bonus? Other than "I come to work every day and work the entire day," which of course only makes them like every other employee and by no means warrants an incentive, most can only muster that they simply believe that they deserve more.

These young people are not necessarily thinking positively – they are presuming positively. The distinction is important. Thinking positively is a conscious decision. You reinforce the positive thinking by associating positive random events with the positive thought. There is a demarcation between the thought and the result brought together by the false association. Presuming positively is an unconscious action. The thought, result, and association are one. One presumes that one's action will have a positive result. The system malfunctions when there is no positive result to associate. Since this originates in the subconscious, one cannot reason why the result was not positive. This may be the outcome of all the childhood conditioning where the individual was in fact the loser, yet was treated like the winner. In other words, winning was the only outcome ever and there lies the root of the presumption. I am afraid that many of these young people reared on Positive Thinking will have a sad and disappointing life. They will never be fully satisfied with any reason for losing.

We have all felt the effects of the negative power of positive thinking in one way or another whether we realize it or not. It is so dangerous and misleading – particularly when it comes down from management. It can manifest itself in a number of ways. Copious amounts of motivational and inspirational framed posters using aphorisms from dead sages (e.g., "Challenges are what make life interesting; overcoming them is what makes life meaningful") are a red flag for sure. But run for your life if the quotes are painted on the wall.

Another manifestation is the motivational speaker. A few years ago, the firm had this motivational speaker come to rally the management team. The team consisted of well educated white collar managers numbering around six hundred. The speaker was the typical positive thinking guru – mixing reality with spirituality and using some change testimonial as proof of the effectiveness of his technique. Then, as with all of these charlatans, he began to appeal to our emotions. In this case, "to fire us up" as they say at rallies.

He was running around screaming, "Ten percent growth - we can do it!" Every so often, he would grab some poor unsuspecting chap from the audience and have him loudly confirm this 10% growth rubbish, as if the louder one screamed, the more likely the gods of fortune would hear it. And heaven forbid if you disagreed with him or showed some prudent skepticism. You not only were spoiling the mood but you were not a team player (that is to say, a disloyal employee).

The crowd would reinforce this disapproval with group taunting. All crowds are the same regardless of their composition. Race, gender education level, and religion seem to matter little. The only matter is crowd size – that is to say, the number of individuals composing the crowd rather than their respective weight. There is a clear inverse correlation between the size of a crowd and its collective good judgment. You can have a crowd of ten thousand grannies and convince them that burning their local office of the AARP is a good idea.

The farce disguised as a rally occurred three weeks before Lehman Brothers collapsed. Even the most junior among us knew something was terribly amiss in the markets. Even for those large numbers of ESs who watch CNBC, it was evident the markets were troubled. Jim Cramer, the host of *Mad Money*, had a mental breakdown on live TV a few weeks earlier pleading to the Federal Reserve's Ben Bernanke to save the investment banks. But as fortune well knows, no one can predict with full certainty, and hindsight is 20/20. It was noticeable only in August 2007 that the markets were failing, but it had not yet become glaringly obvious. Perhaps our leaders were being prudent and not jumping to hasty conclusions. What is not forgivable is that our leaders still believed the 10% nonsense even after the fall of Lehman Brothers when there was no doubt what was happening. They held firm to the 10% growth target and held the management team to it – this during the worst economy since the Great Depression. Our leaders would not revise the numbers down even as the world was imploding. They were immune to reason and reality. They simply hoped as Rome burned.

At year end, of course, we missed our targets by the size of the Grand Canyon. First our leaders rationalized that the high targets were set based on the previous year's actual, and that the current year was such an anomaly that accurately forecasting was beyond anyone's ability. They rationalized that everyone forecasted incorrectly from economists to pundits – even the Federal Reserve got it wrong. But our leaders failed to realize that their primary mistake was not poor forecasting (everyone forecasts poorly and only the few lucky ones get it right).

Their primary mistake can be attributed to the problem of Ideological Immunity. The more knowledge one has amassed and the more accepted the idea, the more confidence one has in the idea. One then becomes immune to new ideas that do not corroborate the old idea. This is likely to have been the case with our leaders. I do not know with certainty, but I suspect our leaders used historical data to devise this 10% growth target. They extrapolated from the data that the current year would be 10% greater than the previous given the linear growth pattern. At minimum, there would be growth given that there had always been some growth over the prior years. The leaders socialized this target with an outside consultant who, for a substantial fee, validated it – probably using the same method that our leaders used to devise the target. Our leaders, using the consultant's report as a sanity check, then all agreed to the 10% growth forecast. And that was that. Going forward, any reason we were not trending to meet the target had to do with the failure of the employees. Nothing was going to change their position – nothing until the fiscal year was over and it was evident the target was indubitably wrong.

As the crisis began to wane, our gray-haired leaders extolled their great leadership abilities. They had clearly seen the crisis looming and had taken the necessary precautions to help manage us through it. It was only with their great leadership that we survived. The ill-conceived 10% target was never seen or heard of again – as if it never was. A clear case of the negative power of positive thinking with hindsight bias – mixed with equals part hubris and arrogance. We were just lucky to have survived.

I often think about those turkeys who actually tried to meet the 10% target. In other words, those that drank the Kool-Aid. I am sure their fate was not as tragic as the Jonestown community's but a Stoic sage might think otherwise. I suspect most of the turkeys probably failed miserably and for the lucky few (or perhaps the unlucky few) that did meet or exceed the target, my guess is that it was not well aligned with their effort. In other words, they received little or nothing in monetary compensation for their hard work. But it was not for lack of desire to reward – there just was not anything to hand out at year's end. It is better to be an average performer in a good market that a stellar performer in a bad one – a very valuable lesson indeed. I am sure that these turkeys' heroics were soon forgotten and I suspect that the bad taste lingers for them knowing that they sacrificed their personal and family life for nothing more than a pat on the back.

I click my mouse on the icon that brings me to my performance metrics dashboard. My numbers look impressive over yesterday. Ron must have been more eager than I initially thought. Perhaps this simple act of entering the lead into the system is enough to secure us the win. My numbers do look good and at least for the moment, I feel good.

Suggested Reading/Resources

Sham: How the Self-Help Movement Made America Helpless

BY STEVE SALERNO

Profiles the gurus and philosophies of the self-help and actualization movement (SHAM), points out the frauds and fallacies respectively and ultimately, why they are a waste of money. In addition, Steve posted an essay on the fallacy of positive thinking in the *eSkeptic* newsletter called "Positively Misguided: The Myths & Mistakes of the Positive Thinking Movement," www.skeptic.com/eskeptic/09-04-15/

The Demon Haunted World: Science as a Candle in the Dark

BY CARL SAGAN

A beautifully written defense of science and testable hypothesis in our modern age of pseudoscience, New Age thinking, and religious extremism. Sagan warns of the dangers when science is replaced by unreason.

CHAPTER 10 - 6:30 PM – CHECKING OUT

"Believing in progress does not mean believing that any progress has yet been made." --Franz Kafka

The day has gone by like it always does – it creeps slowly until it is over and then you wonder where the time has gone and why you have gotten so little accomplished. My train departs at 7:01 but I know it is wishful thinking that I will make it. My bosses stand as sentinels guarding the exits. They make a mental tally of those who leave earlier than they do. We just sit anxiously waiting for the ESs to call it a day.

I open up my timesheet to record my time for the day. I find this ritual quite annoying but I can appreciate the need to account for one's time in the consulting world. However, I think daily time reporting is a bit overzealous. What is one to do with this information? Clients are not invoiced daily and anyone who runs their business on a day-to-day basis is exceedingly simple-minded.

I also struggle with the weekly and monthly forecasting requirement. Unless I am on some long-term engagement, I find it difficult to forecast what I will be doing so far out. I suspect this is true with everyone who has an inkling of the randomness of life. I usually just allot time based on no particular reason. Thinking about it too much does not improve the accuracy, so why bother trying to devise some elaborate forecasting model? I hope leadership understands the difficulty and attempts to adjust for it. If not, their projections will be inaccurate. This may be the case as we are lambasted on occasion by group email for our poor forecasting ability. So much so, we are now measured against our ability to forecast – as if the threat of measurement will improve the forecasting. It is so stupid.

It is ironic how accountants are good at accounting for some things and not others. They can count all kinds of widgets and thingamajigs without missing a beat. It is the same with line managers. Everything always ticks and ties at the end of the day. They know exactly how much they are up or down. Client-facing professionals are no different. Most can account for their customer's assets better than the customer. It is extraordinary. If only these turkeys accounted for their life like they do for their business. They would realize how leveraged they are and how deep their deficit. One can only deficit spend before the system collapses. So obvious and so oblivious. They keep squandering as if they are whole. The donuts and disgraces add up. Put that one in the bank.

It is only Monday but I am already thinking about my plans for the weekend. It is ironic that the weekend is for pastimes and that the work week is for living. Should not work be for passing time and weekends for living? I enjoy living on the weekend. I call it creative indolence. Not the kind of indolence where one sits on the couch, snacks on chips and chugs brew while watching the boob tube. Rather, the kind spent with family on activities that serve no other purpose than to make the family happy. Small carnivals with a few merry-go-rounds or a walk in a nature preserve are good starting points.

I understand the need for weekends. The tension from the week needs to be relieved by recreation. It is a time to check out. It is strange that only a few days to the weekend can seem a lifetime away. I think this perception is from knowing that the weekdays are filled with innumerable obstacles before the weekend's safe harbor. But even weekends are threatened to be just like weekdays. People believe they are in leisure, but in fact it is just idle busyness. They have BlackBerry on the mind even on the sacred weekends.

We need to resist. For now though, I can only muster energy for tomorrow. I wonder how it will differ from today. Will we win the work or will we lose? What are the consequences of each? Are all of these daily happenings poisons that make me weaker or tests that make me stronger? Perhaps they are both – one part of me weakens as another part strengthens. A net zero effect.

I never planned for my life to be like this. I sit and wonder, how did I get here? I used to think life was like the children's game book "Choose Your Own Adventure" – that I could choose my next course of action. It was as simple as a turn of a page. I think this may be true with the smaller things in life – the things like "What should I have for breakfast?" But with the larger things, we have far less control. I feel like we are all just swept away on a raging river, holding onto nothing but a small tree branch.

For me, the river is rough and I almost drown with each dunk, but I'm never under water long enough to expire. The river just takes me – it does not even know where. Its only purpose is to flow. For now, the river is calm. I gently flow in the corporate world. One day the river may rage again and then who knows where it will take me – perhaps smashed on a jagged rock or washed ashore on a gentle beach. The current goes against everything we desire – certainty, control, and simplicity. We strive for this and delude ourselves that we can fight the current. It is not so – nothing is certain, no one really is in full control, and nothing is simple.

My eyes are tired and I have a pain between them that refers outwards to my temples. Maybe I need more caffeine. But I do not like to drink coffee after 5 p.m. If I do, my heart races at midnight when lying still in bed. I think I just need more rest. I find myself in the middle of the night, stiff as a board – flexing my muscles with fist and jaw clenched. Although I am sleeping, my body is not resting. My mind is not resting either. My dreams are just simulations of the day but in strange abstracts. The images change but the mood is the same.

I have researched better ways to sleep. Aside from the obvious
(caffeine being one), there may be other factors that contribute. I
discovered that my mattress is coated with a flame retardant chemical coating to prevent, I assume, my bed from burning in the event
I spontaneously combust. But in all seriousness, it was to address
the risk of smokers who fall asleep with a cigarette in their hand.
There are studies that question the safety of these chemicals with
some states choosing to ban them.[23] The rhetoric does not add
up – put the safety of every sleeping American in danger for the
few morons who die from smoking in bed (ironically, this actually
happened to a distant relative who, frankly, was a bit off). It just
does not add up – but I suppose rhetoric does not have to. Maybe
I am having an allergic reaction that is not allowing my body to
fully rest.

Some say that electrosmog may also be negatively affecting sleep.
Electrosmog is the invisible electromagnetic radiation resulting
from the use of wireless technology, power supplies, home appliances, etc. Studies suggest that some people may be hypersensitive
to this energy.[24] I recently moved my cordless phone away from
bed and took to charging my cell phone in the basement. But who
really knows – there are competing studies on the safety on these
devices as well.

Regardless of what it is, it seems that with each advancement we
make there is a larger number of significant negative drawbacks
(many, I am sure, that we have not yet identified) – most never conceived of by the inventor. With all our technology we are not that
far removed from our ancestral chimp. I cannot help but to think
of that *Far Side* cartoon where a general is showing an audience of
lower ranking generals a slide show. The slide is displaying a mush-
room cloud. The caption reads, "Now this next slide, gentlemen,
demonstrates the awesome power of our twenty megaton ... for
crying out loud! Not again!" The slide is upside-down.

Whether we intended it or not, we designed a world where we are only progressing in the ways in which we destroy. We create without truly understanding and appreciating the complexity inherent in nature. Nature is only encapsulated in simplicity. Inside it is full of complexity. We have only the faintest of understanding of this. This misunderstanding has relegated nature to the role of janitor. We leave a trail of messes and spills for it to clean up.

I need to get out of the office. The ESs are not budging and I am sure to miss the train. It is so much easier to leave for the day the earlier one actually leaves. At 3 p.m., it looks as though you may be off to a client meeting. But at 5, 6, or 7 p.m. – the intent is so clear. I get up and walk over to Victor's cubicle and he is nowhere to be found. I see all of his stuff – even his laptop. I slap myself in the face. I need to get out of here too. I decide to just leave my jacket, umbrella, work bag and laptop in the office. It will appear that I am still at work and my wandering will not raise any red flags.

I head to the elevator. I have this strange excitement inside of me. The exact opposite of the morning when I felt warning signals. It is like the feeling I think Morgan Freeman's Red character felt at the end of the *Shawshank Redemption* –"I find I'm so excited, I can barely sit still or hold a thought in my head. I think it's the excitement only a free man can feel, a free man at the start of a long journey whose conclusion is uncertain. I hope I can make it across the border."

I stand in the elevator bank and excessively click the "down" button. I wait and hope no one spots me. I hope the elevator door does not open and discharge an ES returning from the cafeteria with a late night dinner order. That will be my excuse if questioned – "Half day?… No sir, just grabbing some dinner." The elevator rings and the door opens. It is empty. I get on and click the "L" button. The door closes and I make my way down. It expresses – Yes! I exit and I make my way to the lobby door. I am trying to refrain from running and my walk has morphed into that awkward speed walking form with my hips waddling like a duck and my arms pumping like an engine. There is a bustle of people, but no one that I recognize, but more importantly, no one that recognizes me. I leave.

I make my way outside. Thank goodness the rain has stopped. I hasten my speed walk into a slow jog. The sidewalks are thick with tourists, so I zig and zag with the occasional barrel like a running back on fourth and goal from the eight yard line. I make my way into Grand Central at the 47th Street underground passage, through the vestibule, and down the steep stairs. I reach the lowest level and stop to look at the electronic track assignment board. I am on track 109. I have two minutes before departure. I race through the maze of passageways like an escape from the circles of hell. I tunnel my way down the ramp to the lower concourse. I am huffing but not out of breath. I make it to the platform when the bell of the door shutting rings. I jump on.

The door closes. I am sweating and breathing heavily. My blue shirt evidences my sweat with the contrast between light and dark blue patches. I scan the car – no seats – not even the middle is open. I am forced to stand – but it is OK. At least I am on my way home. I notice the same depressed look on people's faces from the morning but their sleepiness has transformed to exhaustion. Everyone is reading either the *Post* or *Daily News*. No brain cells left to process material harder than fourth-grade level. As we begin to move, I can hear the conductor clicking tickets on the other end of the car. They never miss a one.

The train chugs along. The lights flicker on and off intermittently. As we hit full throttle, we emerge from the tunnel to the raised tracks. The city is beautiful at night. The lights from the street and buildings are a surreal backdrop. I cannot wait to get home. I know it sounds clichéd (which of course is also a cliché), but my kids always run to the door when I get home. My wife is typically exhausted and happy to see me. I think it is love coupled with the relief of knowing that I will soon give the kids a bath and put them to sleep. These thoughts make me happy. I cannot help but feel sorry for the ESs. They have chosen to crawl through a thousand indignities to reach the crowning indignity, but in the end, they will realize that the object of their toil was their epitaph – nothing more. I want more than a calendar – more than just an epitaph – more than nothing to show that I have lived.

Suggested Reading/Resources

The Far Side

BY GARY LARSON

One of the first compilations of *Far Side* cartoons but thank goodness, not the last. A couple of *Far Side* cartoons a day help to lower blood pressure. They should do a study on that.

Life in the Cubicle

BY DUDLEY DAWSON

www.examiner.com/life-the-cubicle-in-national/dudley-dawson

Contains a large number of hilarious vignettes on the absurdities of the job including the "12 books to curb a child's enthusiasm before they enter the workforce" and "Unwritten rules of the office: Elevator etiquette."

Postscript

People who have read my book often ask if I have any advice on how they can better align with nature. As I stated before, I am not a self-help guru so I am not comfortable being prescriptive. In order to provide any advice, I need to know more. A lot depends such as what is one's goal – health, environment, etc.? But the question, "What are we to do (or not to do)?" is fair. Therefore, I will present my point of view based simply on where we may have been as humans some 10,000 years ago. The following bulleted list can be used as a kind of measure to gauge how far we have strayed from our natural state. Many of these suggestions were the norm for humans 10,000 years ago. However, a word of caution – our ancestors came from different geographies and therefore evolved somewhat differently. These are in many cases just generalizations, and so again, it all kind of depends.

Work

- Choose to be a generalist specialist. One does not have all the upside benefits (top salary) but one is shielded from the many drawbacks of unexpected events (obsolescence). [25]

- Work in fits and spurts. Moderation (constant light work without a break) is not natural. We evolved to be at rest with spontaneous episodes of physical intensity.

- Find work where you can move and not just sit all day.

- Allow your work to be scalable (that is, to make money when you are not there). However, unless the scalable work can financially support you immediately (you wrote an award winning screenplay), protect your downside risk with non-scalable work such as a 9-5 salaried job.[26]

- Ultimately however, you are not entirely free if you are working for someone else. Voluntary slavery is still slavery. If you are happy working for someone else, then you are a happy slave. This includes people that own their own businesses. They are slaves to their businesses and customers. They perhaps have it worse than an employee. Most business owners that I know work fourteen-hour days, seven days a week. Tell me, how is that freedom? The foundation of freedom is self-sufficiency without fear.

Food

- Try to eat foods that have not been pre- or post-processed. Many processed foods contain chemicals. Do not trust advertisements that claim a food does not contain a certain chemical substance. It typically does but under a very different name. For example, monosodium glutamate (MSG) is also referred to as calcium glutamate, natrium glutamate, yeast extract, anything "hydrolyzed," calcium caseinate, sodium caseinate, yeast food, yeast nutrient, autolyzed yeast, among many other names[27].

- Eat organic fruits, berries, nuts, and vegetables whenever possible and preferably raw. Raw food supporters maintain that raw foods contain enzymes needed for digestion and other metabolic functions and are destroyed when heated.

The theory is that along with digestive enzymes produced by the body, raw foods, when consumed, aid digestion with the enzymes inherent in the raw food. These additional enzymes reduce the burden on the body during digestion by reducing the number of enzymes the body has to produce. [28]

- Ensure organic food is grown in the U.S. Most meat and produce sourced from outside the U.S., even if it is labeled organic, is treated with DDT and other harmful pesticides prior to transport in order to pass pest inspection as required by the USDA Animal and Plant Health Inspection Service (APHIS). In 2008, the FDA reported that approximately 4.7% of imported fresh fruits and vegetables sampled had violations (approximately 28% had detectable residue but did not warrant a violation). However, the FDA represents that their testing should not be considered statistical or random given that they use a "focused testing" approach. The testing involved the following: 3,655 samples representing food shipments from 93 countries were tested with about 1/3 representing shipments from Mexico and China. Fifty-three countries were not tested. Of the 3,655 samples, 2,610 were in the fruit and vegetable categories that represented approximately 100 types of fruits and vegetables. That is an average of just 26 units sampled per fruit/vegetable. [29] Given that the U.S. imports billions a year in fresh fruits and vegetables, the FDA testing does not provide me a lot of comfort in the safety of our imports.

- Whether humans should eat meat or not is unclear. Certain humans live almost exclusively on meat (the Inuit [30]). If this is the case, certainly the opposite could be true (tribes that lived exclusively on caloric dense fruits and nuts). If one feels the need to eat meat, choose organic beef from grass fed cattle, and non-farmed fish whenever possible. Healthy chicken, pork, and eggs are more difficult to come by given that terms like "cage free" and "free range" are little more than deceptive marketing techniques.[31] Try not to eat meat at every meal. Too much meat (as well as breads, sweets, and acidic drinks like coffee) creates an acidic ph in the blood which requires the body to leach its own alkalizing minerals to rebalance to acid-base homeostasis (i.e., neutral).[32] Stagger meat consumption as if it were scarce, like an animal you hunted in the wilderness.

- Eat fats from natural sources such as nuts and avocados (for meat eaters, from organic sources given that factory farm animal's contain unnaturally high fat content). Oils are processed so avoid.

- Avoid grains and legumes when possible as most humans have not evolved to eat these foods. In addition, in the case of grains, most come only highly processed. Grains include corn. (Yes, corn is a grain and not a vegetable. Ever have corn bread?) And legumes include peanuts (the word "nut" is a misnomer).

- Always avoid dairy (milk, butter, yogurt, cheese, cream, ice cream) and dairy derivatives (whey, casein, lactate). Dairy was not consumed by Paleolithic humans (unless of course they had refrigerators). There are a host of other issues beyond just the growth hormone issue. These include allergies, effects of chemicals (dioxin) and antibiotics in dairy, safety of homogenization, irritable bowel syndrome, and arthritis to name just a few.[33]

- Avoid seafood that is farmed (in particular imported/non-U.S. seafood)[34]. Farmed sea animals suffer through similar conditions to factory farm animals and therefore suffer from the same defects.[35]

- Eat wild seafood that is sourced from lakes or near the shoreline. Our ancestors did not fish out in the middle of the ocean and probably never ate these types of fish in great quantity. One must, however, consider the source as many local streams and lakes are polluted. Chemicals and other waste carry over to the fish and aquatic life they support.

- Allow at least 12 hours from when the last meal is eaten for the day and the first meal is eaten the following day. Think of it like a mini-fast. This affords the digestive system a restorative break (physiological rest), allows catabolic processes to function (autophagy is the process in which cells break down damaged cells), and retrains the body to use alternate sources of fuel (ketones are an alternate energy source to glucose that are not used unless glucose stores are depleted). [36] Eat the last meal of the day three to four hours prior to bedtime to help improve sleep.

- Be wary of anything advertised as natural. Among hundreds of examples is carrageenan. It is natural because it is derived from seaweed yet it can cause upset stomach and also has been associated with gastrointestinal cancer.[37]

- Avoid caffeine in general. Caffeine can be found in coffee and chocolate and is a stimulant that forces the body to expend energy to excrete. In other words, it is a waste of energy.[38]

- Avoid all condiments. Many are full of sodium and contain stimulants. This includes olives and pickles that pack shocking levels of sodium in each morsel.

- Eat on a varied schedule and varied amounts. The body is not a machine that is designed to be fueled at predetermined times of the day.

- Avoid drinking any alcohol. It destroys cells on contact and forces the body to expend energy to excrete. In other words, it is also a waste of energy.[39]

- Take small steps to achieve the targeted goal of adding and removing certain foods. Dairy should be removed first. Try it for a week. See how much less mucous and phlegm you have. You will be pleasantly surprised.

Fitness

- Avoid supplementation. Supplements are a product of human arrogance. There is so much that is not known about human biology and chemistry. Every year some new supplement is discovered – this alone is clearly a warning of our lack of knowledge. Think about the thousands of nutrients that have not been discovered and the complex relationship between them. Tampering with one may cause a ripple effect through the network of all nutrients.[40] We just do not know. It is better to get nutrients from real food and from the outdoors like we were designed (vitamin D from the sun, calcium from spinach, etc.).

- Get outside as often as possible including when exercising. Who needs an indoor gym membership when the world is a gym? Outdoor exercising more closely exhibits a real world environment that will improve your ability to handle real world situations.

- When exercising outdoors, be careful of the time of day and where outdoors you work out as air pollution varies.[41] Mornings are best.

- When exercising, focus efforts based on usefulness in everyday life – exercise bicycles are not useful unless one is training to compete in a pedaling race. If interested in self-defense training as exercise, focus on a system that is also practical in the real world.[42]

- Level of effort is important. Frequent exercise at high intensity can lead to overtraining and can weaken and damage the body unless one is training like an athlete. Athletes live a lifestyle where they eat properly and give themselves time to recover through increased physical rest and by incorporating certain types of restorative training methods. For example, periodization is a training technique that shifts an athlete's exercises leading up to the competition so as not to over-train one particularly ability. [43]

- Incorporate variety as well – it is more fun and will continue to challenge your body's adaptive capability.

- Do not drink sports drinks or even worse, milk, before, during, or after exercising. [44] Instead drink clean water. If the exercise routine is particularly intense, drink either coconut water or make your own sports drink (blend a banana and a celery stick in 12 ounces of water).

- If you have not exercised in a very long time and are worried about injury, start slowly and with progressions. Before strength exercises, begin with daily light static stretches to increase your range of motion (you have no strength in a certain range if you are too tight to even move within that range). Sitting all day encourages poor posture and tightness of muscles and fascia. Incorporate self-myofascial release (a type of self massage) using a foam roller to supplement stretching. Focus stretching and myofascial release on targeted areas including thoracic spine (will help to loosen shoulders and chest), hamstrings and hip flexors. Slowly incorporate key body weight exercises (push-ups, inverted row and squats) and dynamic stretches (full back stretch, dynamic chest stretch, and leg swings).

Personal Care

- Do not use an alarm clock to wake up. Let your body naturally wake up. It will tell you how much sleep you need.

- Drink and bathe in filtered water. There are chemicals in our water supply to fortify the water (fluoride) and to clean the water (chlorine). These chemicals may negatively affect the body when ingested and breathed.[45] [46] There are also traces of pharmaceuticals in our water that are not filtered in municipal filtration stations.[47] Use your own filters for drinking and bathing or buy filtered water for drinking.

- Avoid unnatural products on your body. This includes most soaps, toothpastes, deodorants, shampoos, lotions, and other cosmetics. Many of these products contain substances that are absorbed through the skin and have been associated with various types of cancer. These substances include any product with an ingredient such as phthalates, parabens, phenols and fragrance.[48]

- Drink when you are thirsty (preferably water but coconut water is good too). The eight glasses of water a day mantra is a myth and has no sound basis.[49] Perhaps it was recommended to offset the gross amounts of sodium typically consumed in the standard diet. Or perhaps it is necessary to improve digestion when eating bread as a primary food staple (put a slice of bread in a glass of water and see how much water gets absorbed. Now imagine that is your stomach.)

Suggested Reading/Resources

Movnat

www.movnat.com

The official website of Movnat. Contains interviews with Erwan Le Corre and his blogs. Check out the video the *Workout The World Forgot*. It is breathtaking.

The Paleo Solution: The Original Human Diet

BY ROBB WOLF

A complete reference guide on eating and living Paleo. Offers a theory on why humans need to eat meat, with a deep dive into the inner workings of the human body. Ignore the testimonials and other marketing material puffery.

The Live Food Factor

BY SUSAN SCHENCK AND VICTORIA BIDWELL

A comprehensive reference book on eating raw, but contains both science and pseudoscience. Offers various points of view from vegetarian to fruitarian. Ignore the testimonials and other marketing material puffery.

Brazilian Jiu-Jitsu: Theory and Technique

BY RENZO GRACIE, ROYLER GRACIE, JOHN DANAHER, KID PELIGRO

Provides the history and evolution of Brazilian Jiu-Jitsu as well as step-by-step instructions on a number of techniques.

Sustainable Table

www.sustainabletable.org

Website devoted to promoting the positive shift toward local, small-scale sustainable farming. The site offers information on the various harmful effects of factory farming and benefits of sustainable agriculture.

The New Evolution Diet

BY ARTHUR DE VANY

www.arthurdevany.com

This book will be published late December 2010 and will go into depth on the science of Evolutionary Fitness. Art's website contains a ton of valuable content on a broad range of topics including interesting and provocative subjects such as Death by Exercise, Intermittent Fasting, and Uncertainty. Content is posted frequently (around twice a week) and Art provides empirical support for many of his assertions. Archives are searchable. Membership is approximately $40 for an annual subscription. It is well worth it.

Glossary

Chiron's Gate: The predicate to freedom. Requires both self-sufficiency and absence of fear.

Corporate Positive Thinking Fallacy: Form of positive thinking in the workplace based on one's relative position within in the organization, from subordinates (self-grandeur), peers (wishful thinking), and bosses (motivational aka Kool-Aid). It has its roots in the Ludic Fallacy and our normative standards that encourage it.

Dairy Delusion: Irrational belief that dairy is healthy; moreover, natural to consume. A symptom of the delusion is after one is presented with the irrefutable facts of the negative health and environmental impact of dairy, one switches from regular whole milk to organic non-fat milk..

Data Quality Fallacy: Using data of unknown quality to support reporting and analysis without recognizing the potential negative implications that doing so may have on the reporting and analysis. More generally, the false premise that data are complete and accu-rate.

Electrosmog: The invisible electromagnetic radiation resulting from the use of wireless technology, power supplies, home appliances, etc. The effects on the body are unknown and research is contradictory (think discourse on cellular phone usage and cancer).

Empty Suit: The physical manifestation of the Dunning-Kruger effect (the illusory superiority of the incompetent) with the additional components of power and authority.

Flip-Flop Engagement Economics: When the sales team determines the effort of an engagement (people and duration) by reverse engineering the client's fee expectation rather than determining the effort of an engagement by more sound means (previous experience) and then providing the client with a fee estimate. This is the greatest fear of all delivery teams.

Ludic Fallacy: Term coined by Nassim Taleb to describe the error of thinking of those that base the study of chance on the narrow world of games and dice. It applies more broadly to anyone who confuses games with real life. This includes good corporate citizens who play by the rules but are caught off guard when they lose their jobs and those investors that were financially ruined when Madoff broke the law (laws are just a set of rules, like a game) and made off with their money (see *Turkey*).

Modern Business Ethics: The use of rhetoric combined with Machiavellianism and Cyrenaic hedonism in the domains of science and business. Modern ethics does not concern itself with what may be right or wrong; rather, all outcomes (ends) are valued based on gratification (pleasure is paramount), amount (more is better) and timeliness of results (instant returns are best). Any action or omis-sion (means) necessary to achieve an outcome is deemed available as an option. The chosen means is never fully known to most because it is obfuscated to the public with rhetoric and other forms of window dressing (e.g., displays of charitable giving to demonstrate altruism when in fact, it is just a sleight of hand trick to mask a greater deceit). Exemplified by the actions of Goldman Sachs and Monsanto (including alumni)

Retrograde Effect: The effects from modern inventions that optimize one area but weaken many more. The appearance is progress but with the hidden net effect of increased fragility.

Rhetoric: Language used to persuade that does not need to be logical or true – just convincing. Rhetoric is the preferred communication method of the Empty Suit because a fallacy communicated verbally (particularly narrative fallacies) is difficult to detect and disprove in the moment it is spoken.

Stationary Motion Phenomenon: The appearance that everything is moving faster than you are, and the feeling that this has always occurred and will continue to occur. It is manifested as the percep-tion that you are always in the slowest line, or that you always lose the convenient parking spot to the other guy. Similar to the Tread-mill Effect (aka "keeping up with the Joneses"). The difference is that in the former people perceive their situations as unfair, and in the latter they measure their happiness against that of others.

Turkey: Person who is fooled by positive reinforcement. Their confidence increases with each positive event whilst not knowing the intent of the reinforcer (which of course can always change). This exposes the person to negative surprises like a turkey fattened for Thanksgiving. It can also be applied with the negative (decrease in confidence) but in either case, the person is surprised and unprepared. Usage coined by Nassim Taleb.

Unpleasant Weather Condition Effect: When slight unpleasantries of weather disproportionately affect the pace of the modern world. This is caused by humans disconnecting with (and fearing) nature.

Wandering's Chasm: The gap between what "is" (our modern world) and what "ought to be" (nature/our nature). The Stoic's aim is to bridge this gap with wisdom, to become not only free (see Chiron's Gate) but an *antislave*, to be empowered by one's shackles and the shackles of others. This is what it means to be a sage.

ACKNOWLEDGMENTS

This book was a pleasure to write but it did not write itself. Obviously, I had a large part to do with it but there were a number of important people who were critical to its development as well.

I would like to thank my wife – who also moonlights as my editor. You really shaped the flow and the voice of the characters when there was little flow and just an academic voice. Your gentle persua-sion also helped soothe the sting when I had to remove well written text that served no purpose other than it being well written.

My friends also assisted in the development of the book – each in their own unique ways and more often than not, like me, during off hours. My advisor Marcus Aurelius provided me direction on where the story should go and arrangements of the section. Nazare Rio gave me excellent feedback and encouragement during the last steps of writing. These are often the times when you hit sticking points and when encouragement is the difference between nothing and something great. I thank the scholar Darren Walk who provided me the encouragement and feedback when the book was just a twinkle in my eye. And last, but not least, I owe a big debt to Philo Levine who provided the micro and macro levels of feedback required to give the book its polish – particularly the sections that lacked clarity and cohesiveness, of which there were many.

NOTES

[1] "The Pillars," Movnat, http://movnat.com/philosophy/the-pillars/ (accessed 11/2/2010).

[2] "Breast Cancer," http://www.notmilk.com/b.html (accessed 11/2/2010).

[3] "Great Outdoors: How Our Natural Health Service Uses Green Space To Improve Wellbeing," Faculty of Public Health, http://www.fph.org.uk/uploads/bs_great_outdoors.pdf (accessed 11/2/2010).

[4] Hermanussen, Michael. "Stature of Early Europeans," Hormones: International Journal of Endocrinology and Medicine http://www.hormones.gr/preview.php?c_id=127 (accessed 11/2/2010).

[5] Ibid.

[6] "Diets Bad For The Teeth Are Also Bad For The Body: Dental disease may be a wake-up call that your diet is harming your body," Science Daily (July 12, 2009),

http://www.sciencedaily.com/releases/2009/07/090709170807.htm (accessed 11/2/2010).

[7] Diamond, Jared. "The Worst Mistake In The History Of The Human Race," Discover-May 1987, http://www.ditext.com/diamond/mistake.html (accessed 11/2/2010).

[8] Dawkins, Richard. *The Selfish Gene*, Oxford University Press, http://www.arvindguptatoys.com/arvindgupta/selfishgene-dowkins.pdf (accessed 11/2/2010).

[9] "BSE: Disease control & eradication - Causes of BSE: The BSE Inquiry Report," UK Department for Environment, Food and Rural Affairs (Defra), http://www.defra.gov.uk/foodfarm/farmanimal/diseases/atoz/bse/controls-eradication/causes.htm (accessed 11/2/2010).

[10] "Cruel Confinement," The Humane Society of the United States, http://www.humanesociety.org/issues/confinement_farmhttp://www.humanesociety.org/issues/confinement_farm

(accessed 11/2/2010).

[11] "An HSUS Report: Human Health Implications of Non-Therapeutic Antibiotic Use in Animal Agriculture," Humane Society of the United States, http://www.hsus.org/web-files/PDF/farm/HSUS-Human-Health-Report-on-Antibiotics-in-Animal-Agriculture.pdf (accessed 11/2/2010).

[12] Garrett, Laurie. "The Next Pandemic? Probable Cause," *Foreign Affairs*, July/August 2005.

[13] De Vany, Arthur. "Art's Essay on Evolutionary Fitness," Arthur De Vany's Evolutionary Fitness http://www.arthurdevany.com/categories/20091026 (accessed 11/2/2010).

[14] "Wisconsin Cow Sets New National Milk Production Record," Holstein Association USA, http://www.holsteinusa.com/news/press_release2010.jsp#pr2010_04 (accessed (11/2/2010) (converted 72,170 pounds of milk to 8,648 gallons of milk and divided by 365 days = ~23 gallons per day).

[15] "Animal Welfare," sustainable table, http://www.sustainabletable.org/issues/animalwelfare/#cows (accessed 11/2/2010).

[16] Dunning, David and Kruger, Justin. "Unskilled and Unaware of It: How Difficulties in Recognizing One's Own Incompetence Lead to Inflated Self-Assessments," *Journal of Personality and Social Psychology 1999*, Vol. 77, No. 6.] 121-1134.

[17] Ibid.

[18] "The Worst American CEOs of All Time," CNBC.com, http://www.cnbc.com/id/30502091/Portfolio_s_Worst_American_CEOs_of_All_Time (accessed 11/2/2010).

[19] Carlson, Nicholas. "10 Years After AOL-Time Warner, Gerald Levin Says He's Sorry," *Business Insider,* http://www.businessinsider.com/10-years-after-aol-time-warner-gerald-levin-says-hes-sorry-2010-1 (accessed 11/2/2010).

[20] "Dick Fuld Testimony: No Apologies Here," WSJ BLOGS Deal Journal (September 1, 2010), http://blogs.wsj.com/deals/2010/09/01/dick-fuld-testimony-no-apologies-here (accessed 11/2/2010).

[21] "PBS Dr. David Graham shows how FDA managers tried to silence him for indicating Vioxx unsafe," Current TV (December 19, 2007), http://current.com/green/88795960_pbs-dr-david-graham-shows-how-fda-managers-tried-to-silence-him-for-indicating-vioxx-unsafe.htm (accessed 11/2/2010).

[22] Freedman, David H. "Lies, Damned Lies, and Medical Science," The Atlantic (November 2010), http://www.theatlantic.com/magazine/print/2010/11/lies-damned-lies-and-medical-science/8269 (accessed 11/2/2010).

[23] "Maine Legislature Votes to Ban Toxic 'Deca' Flame Retardant." The Natural Resources Council of Maine, http://www.nrcm.org/news_detail.asp?news=1568 (accessed 11/2/2010).

[24] Segell, Michael. "Is 'electrosmog' harming our health?" msnbc. msn.com, http://www.msnbc.msn.com/id/34509513/ (accessed 11/2/2010).

[25] Taleb, Nassim N. *The Black Swan: The Impact of the Highly Improbable*, (Random House 2010), 371.

[26] Ibid 205-06.

[27] "Types of products that contain MSG," truthinlabeling.org, http://www.truthinlabeling.org/II.WhereIsMSG.html (accessed 11/02/2010).

[28] Howell, Edward "ENZYME NUTRITION: THE FOOD ENZYME CONCEPT," http://sites.commercecreators.com/ folder1394/listing/EnzymeNutrition.pdf (accessed 11/2/2010).

[29] "Pesticide Monitoring Program FY 2008," FDA U.S. Food and Drug Administration, http://www.fda.gov/Food/ FoodSafety/FoodContaminantsAdulteration/Pesticides/ ResidueMonitoringReports/ucm228867.htm   (accessed 11/2/2010).

[30] Heinbecker, Peter. "Studies on the Metabolism of Eskimos," Washington University School of Medicine, St. Louis (July 9, 1928) http://www.jbc.org/content/80/2/461.full.pdf (accessed 11/2/2010).

[31] Foer, Jonathan S. *Eating Animals*, (Back Bay Books 2009), 61.

[32] Edwards, Sharon L. "Pathophysiology of acid base balance: The theory practice relationship" page 3, http://download.journals.elsevierhealth.com/pdfs/journals/0964-3397/ PIIS0964339707000547.pdf (accessed 11/2/2010).

[33] Cohen, Robert. "MILK: A-Z," Vegan London, http://www. veganlondon.co.uk/factsheets/milk.pdf (11/2/2010).

[34] Main, Emily. "12 Fish You Shouldn't Eat", Rodale.com (Sep 20, 2010) http://www.rodale.com/fish-avoid?page=0%2C0 (accessed 11/2/2010)

[35] Foer, Jonathan S. *Eating Animals*, (Back Bay Books 2009), 189-190.

[36] Cahill Jr., George F. "Fuel Metabolism in Starvation," University of Pennsylvania - School of Medicine (May 2006), http://www.med.upenn.edu/timm/documents/ReviewArticleTIMM2008-9Lazar-1.pdf (accessed 11/2/2010).

[37] "Review of Harmful Gastrointestinal Effects of Carrageenan in Animal Experiments," Environmental Health Perspectives Volume 109, Number 10, October 2001, http://ehp.niehs.nih.gov/members/2001/109p983-994tobacman/tobacman-full.html (accessed 11/2/2010).

[38] "Do You Find This Stimulating?," FoodnSport, http://foodnsport.com/blog/articles/do-you-find-this-stimulating.html (accessed 11/2/2010).

[39] Graham, Douglas M. Nutrition and Athletic Performance, *FoodnSport 2008*, 61-66.

[40] Freedman, David H. "Lies, Damned Lies, and Medical Science," *The Atlantic* (November 2010), http://www.theatlantic.com/magazine/print/2010/11/lies-damned-lies-and-medical-science/8269 (accessed 11/2/2010).

[41] Reynolds, Gretchen. "Air pollution holds risks for athletes who exercise outdoors," *New York Times* (July 12, 2007), http://www.nytimes.com/2007/07/12/health/12iht-air.1.6628800.html (accessed 11/2/2010).

[42] Kurz, Thomas. "Self-Defense Tip #14 Selecting a self-defense system—Part I," www.real-self-defense.com, http://www.real-self-defense.com/self_defense_tip_14.html (accessed 11/2/2010).

[43] Kurz, Thomas. "Periodization Made Really Simple" Stadion News, http://www.stadion.com/free/nltr0105.pdf (accessed 11/2/2010).

[44] Graham, Douglas M. Nutrition and Athletic Performance, FoodnSport 2008, 91-94.

[45] Hattersley, Joseph G. "The Negative Health Effects of Chlorine," *The Journal of Orthomolecular Medicine Vol. 15*, 2nd Quarter 2000, http://www.orthomolecular.org/library/jom/2000/articles/2000-v15n02-p089.shtml (accessed 11/2/2010).

[46] "Request for a scientific opinion: Critical review of any new evidence on the hazard profile, health effects, and human exposure to fluoride...," Scientific Committee on Health and Environmental Risks (SCHER), http://ec.europa.eu/health/ph_risk/committees/04_scher/docs/scher_q_084.pdf (accessed 11/2/2010).

[47] Leoning, Carol D. "Area Tap Water Has Traces of Medicines," *Washington Post* (March 10, 2008),

http://www.washingtonpost.com/wp-dyn/content/story/2008/03/09/ST2008030901877.html (accessed 11/2/2010).

[48] Crinnion, Walter J. "Toxic Effects of the Easily Avoidable Phthalates and Parabens," Alternative Medicine Review (September 2010 - Volume 15, Number 3), http://altmedrev.com/sobi2.html?sobi2Task=dd_download&fid=474 (accessed 11/2/2010).

[49] Belliner, Karen. "Fact or Fiction? You Must Drink 8 Glasses of Water Daily," *Scientific American* (June 4, 2009), http://www.scientificamerican.com/article.cfm?id=eight-glasses-water-per-day (accessed 11/2/2010).

INDEX

Lightning Source UK Ltd.
Milton Keynes UK
UKOW04f2100021213

222267UK00017B/902/P